THE CIDER INSIDER

The essential guide to 100 craft ciders to drink now

SUSANNA FORBES

Cover illustration by Tom Frost
Cider illustrations by Sarah Fisher

quadrille

CIDER & PERRY FLAVOUR GUIDE

To help you navigate your way, we have given each cider and perry one of the following flavour descriptions:

PERRY

Of course, its own world. As it should be. Sublime. From lemon-infused wine-like offerings through to elegantly sparkling French numbers that reshaped the cider world.

BRIGHT & FRESH

Where acidity and dry characteristics lead the way, here's where the unsweetened paragons appear alongside those from regions where cider tannins are not the norm.

FRUITY & FUN

A dash of sweetness helps accentuate the fruit in your glass, so here you'll find the keeved ciders, and those backsweetened, whether by Tate & Lyle or apple juice.

RUSTIC & STRUCTURED

Here's where cider tannins rule and the farmyard peeps through the door.

VIVA ESPAÑA

In Spain, cider is a way of thinking. While Spain produces many styles, it's best known for its tangy, sassy food-friendly ciders.

DRAMA & DIFFEENCE

Here's where you find the ciders breaking boundaries. Those embracing hops or flirting with fruits.

ICE MAIDENS

Its own little world, the ice ciders and perries of ciderland.

Throughout history, the documentation of cider has been poor, if not non-existent. The current resurgence in the making, drinking and interest in cider (and perry) has heralded a need to record this vibrant, refreshing new turn of events. This book is a snapshot in time of the variety and qualities of ciders from around the world.

So drop what you are doing, grab a bottle, ease the crown cap or cork off, pour some cider and read about what is happening now.

Join us in this celebration of the greatest drink. It is about to find its way back to the glory days of the 1800s and beyond. Susanna's book *The Cider Insider* is the perfect guide you need to find out about the apple, the orchard, the maker and blender – in short, cider.

Cheers.

Tom Oliver
Oliver's Cider & Perry, Herefordshire

INTRODUCTION

Holding this green-and-red flecked apple in my hand, it's awe-inspiring to think how much such a small and seemingly simple piece of fruit has contributed to the world. Whether you call it *apfelwein*, *sidra*, *sagardoa* or cider, everyone from peasants to presidents has drunk this golden liquid.

But why does cider differ so markedly depending on where you are? Apple and pear trees grow predominantly in two bands above and below the equator, 35–50°N and 30–45°S. Certainly there are style preferences and cultural differences in production but, equally importantly, the difference comes from the genetic fickleness of the apple. Seedlings do not relate to their parents, hence the thousands of different apple varieties.

Genetic analysis around a decade ago confirmed that the domestic apple (*Malus domestica*) is descended from apple cultivars still found in the forests of Kazakhstan (*Malus sieversii*). From there, the apple spread throughout the world, evolving as it went. And that's where the fascination begins.

I began this book with the idea of sharing the beauty of the cider I had discovered when I began exploring its English heartlands a decade or so ago. But the book became more. This odyssey has become the story of communities seeking to reconnect with the depth that a well-crafted cider offers, the sorts of flavours on offer before the mass-market production of cider took over. There's no denying the refreshment potential of cider. But this friendly fruit, with its intricate interplay of sweetness, tang and sometimes tongue-teasing tannins, offers more. Cider deserves to be on your dinner table. To entertain your senses as well as to quench your thirst.

CONTENTS

FOREWORD

Cider resonates with some but for many, it is seemingly hard to define.

At its simplest, it is fermented apple juice. At its best it is a glorious drink, reminiscent of bucolic sun-drenched countryside and orchards. Wassail-blessed trees that usher in the blossom of spring. Then through the growing season of summer sun and rain, swelling the fruit till the autumn harvest sees the orchards once again stripped of apples, to be crushed and pressed so that more cider can be made.

Cider that harnesses the aroma of ripe apples, both flesh and skin, with a depth and intensity of flavour that only apple tannins, acids and sugars can bequeath, is a drink that truly expresses *terroir*, robustness, yet finesse and character.

Susanna has made a determined effort to locate many of these wonderful ciders. Travelling here, there and everywhere, and with the assistance of many cider friends, she has assembled a fine collection from all over the ever-expanding world of cider.

Harnessing her considerable experience of writing about the drinks trade for many years and her own personal quest to make cider with her husband James at Little Pomona in Herefordshire, she is ideally placed to capture this brave new world.

Cider is, after all, apple wine. It oozes *terroir*. Yes, you can transport apples and juice across land and sea, but ultimately cider speaks of the landscape, the climate and the culture from where it emanates. A Kingston Black from Australia will taste different to one from Somerset.

We can all crush apples and leave the juice to ferment naturally. So what makes a great cider? Ultimately it's balance. That interplay between acids, sweetness, texture and tannins. A great cider is also about eliciting subtlety. Coaxing complexity. Knowing when it's right not just to harvest but also when to finish fermenting. What to blend. And when to bottle. Finally, it's allowing the newborn cider the time to come into its own before release. For those who need a brief refresher on the processes turn to page 220.

That's what this book bears witness to: the skills and the knowledge that only time and dedication can bring to bear. This book isn't a historical tome or a '*How to...*' guide. That's covered brilliantly elsewhere – see page 222 for a few of my favourites. This is a snapshot of the scene today, designed to enable you to begin your own quest. To track down the ciders that make you sing. To meet the makers. Perhaps even to inspire you to craft your own cider.

This book is dedicated to all who shared their stories with me – the cidermakers and the orchardists – and their ciders. Relentlessly inspiring, every one deserves your attention. And it's dedicated to you, the reader. This is just the beginning.
Happy hunting...

Susanna Forbes
Little Pomona Orchard & Cidery

ENGLAND, WALES & IRELAND

Nothing quite prepares you for the moment you walk into the final gallery on the ground floor of the Cider Museum in Hereford. You've been welcomed by the friendly staff, gone past some bucolic murals, and smocks for the kids, glanced at an old stone mill. Then you see them: cabinets that glisten with sparkling stemware and cut-glass decanters from the 18th century. Reminders of the time when cider and perry graced the tables of nobility and royalty as well as replenished the workers.

So what happened? Why did cider lose its place at the top table, reverting solely to the rural answer to refreshment? The wars stopped and wine and port came back into vogue. Elsewhere, cider merchants began buying juice and 'lengthening' it. And so the demise continued.

By the time the 21st century arrived, the big players had been so successful at ciders destined to quench the thirst, most of them seemed to have lost sight of the possibilities offered by more complex, orchard-driven ciders.

Except there were always pockets of excellence. Those farmers who continued to ferment a special barrel or two that they kept in the cellar for the family.

Dictated by the varieties in use, two broad styles dominate: the rich, bittersweet/bittersharp-infused ciders favoured by the West Country, and the more

EXPLORE

Cider Museum, Hereford: cidermuseum.co.uk

Cider & Perry Academy: Peter Mitchell, cider-academy.co.uk

National Association of Cider Makers: ciderukcom

National Perry Pear Centre: nationalperry pearcentre.org.uk

South West of England Cidermakers' Association: sweca.org.uk

The Orchard Project: theorchard project.org.uk

Three Counties Cider & Perry Association: thethreecounties ciderandperry association.co.uk

Welsh Cider & Perry Association: welshcider.co.uk

Apple Day, October: commonground.org.uk/apple-day

Blossomtime, Harvestime, The Big Apple Association: bigapple.org.uk

Cider Salon, June: cidersalon.co.uk

Royal Bath & West Show, May/June: bathandwest.com/royal-bath-and-west-show

Andrew Lea: eminent cidermaking authority, cider.org.uk

Bill Bradshaw: cider globetrotter, billbradshaw.co.uk/cider

Gabe Cook: The Ciderologist, theciderologist.com

acid-driven dessert/culinary-fruit ciders of the east. However, there's plenty of crossover, and production and maturation methods vary. Bottle conditioning and traditional – or 'champagne' – method secondary fermentation are regular sights, the bold are adopting keeving, the technique perfected by the French, and mould-breakers – including Oliver's and Hawkes – are happy to blur boundaries.

The majority of the cider producers in this chapter have emerged relatively recently, suggesting perhaps that the UK is on the brink of change. Having said that, one of the oldest producers in the book, Aspall, is our east coast contender, based in Suffolk. As dessert fruit growers and winemakers get involved, so Kent and Hampshire are emerging. Even London. But the majority are west of Winchester. While Dorset starts to reclaim its own identity, Devon and Somerset join the Three County producers to claim the lion's share.

While each cidermaker here takes a distinctively different approach, a pride in the apple is what unites them – in fostering what each variety can produce. This relates similarly across the border in Wales. While climatic conditions may seem similar, it's specific apple varieties that our producers cherish. For Andy Hallett, it's the Monmouthshire apple, Frederick. Cross the Irish Sea and not only do we hear echoes of this, we go one step further, and find a trophy-winning cider crafted from trees hidden in hedgerows.

Perry, meanwhile, continues to be the wild child. Our duo come from trees grown in the perry pear's heartland, Herefordshire. Legend has it that the best perries are made within sight of local landmark, May Hill. Often harvested from centuries-old trees, as elsewhere in Europe, these titans of the orchard world still need championing to ensure they survive.

I write this the day after England's first Cider Salon, held in Bristol, where many of those featured in these pages appeared. It felt like a game changer. Does this herald the start of our cider renaissance? Let's hope so.

OLIVER'S CIDER & PERRY
VINTAGE FINE CIDER, SEASON 2015

region: Herefordshire, England

fruit: bittersweet, bittersharp apple blend

life story: a blend of the best from the previous year's harvest, following a slow natural fermentation and a year in cask; further maturation before release

abv: 6.8%

if you like this: try Yarlington Mill, keeved; At the Hop; Stoke Red; Fine Perry, bottle conditioned

experience: visit Tasting Room, Saturday; Cider Salon, June; Terra Madre, December; Malvern Autumn Show, September; check website and follow social media for news of events

oliversciderand perry.co.uk

Sublime. And inspirational. Tom Oliver's ciders are the contemplative sort. The ones that stun you into a reverie about how such complexity can be coaxed from the humble apple. Except the apple isn't humble in Tom's eyes. He's all about letting the apple speak.

Nowhere is this more evident than in his Vintage Cider. A magical blend crafted from the very best barrels from each harvest, this never arrives until almost two years after the vintage. And that's the other clue to Tom's magic: time. He's not for rushing. 'Patience is the thing that most people struggle with,' he says. 'But I find I can be incredibly patient with cider. Don't bully it, don't rush it. If you give stuff time, it will reward you.'

Tom has been making cider for nearly 20 years, drawing on the heritage of the land he grew up in with a talent and palate that inspire the world.

The true mastery of the cidermaker is in the blending. Like a perfumier, the cidermaker memorises the scent and flavour signature from each barrel, selecting their favourites from that year, marrying them together in the right proportions, before returning them to the barrel for further integration.

The 2015 Vintage Blend is a blend mainly of glorious bittersweets Dabinett and Yarlington Mill, with a splash of aromatic Stoke Red and zesty Foxwhelp. It's still, a golden, smoky nectar, rich with apple skins and the subtlest flourish of vanilla from its time in cask. The layers of eloquent apple notes speak of the Herefordshire orchards from whence they were picked. There's marmalade zest, tart apricots and a tantalising seam of acidity from that bittersharp maestro, Foxwhelp.

Food-friendly it certainly is, but it's also one to just marvel at. You owe it to yourself. And to Tom. Cheers.

OLIVER'S
VINTAGE
FINE CIDER
DRY
SEASON 2015

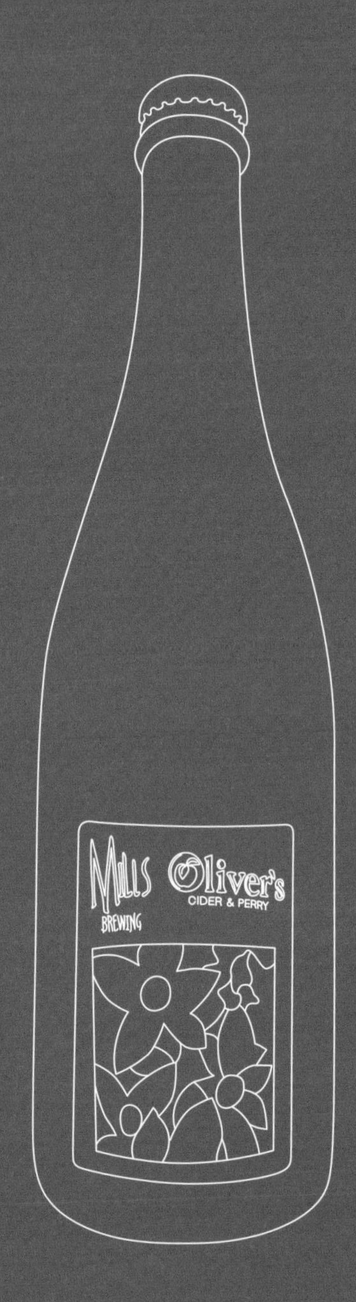
MILLS
BREWING
Oliver's
CIDER & PERRY

MILLS BREWING/OLIVER'S CIDER
FOXBIC

And now for something that truly deserves the 'Drama & Difference' description: Foxbic. This is a collaboration between two of the most creative minds in the business, the intuitive flavour maestro that is Tom Oliver (see page 10), in love with lambics almost as much as apples and pears, and the wild kid himself, Jonny Mills, for whom natural fermentations are the only way to go.

Tom was arguably the first in Blighty to straddle the cider/beer boundary with style when he collaborated with Thornbridge and Brooklyn to craft 2015's runaway hit, The Serpent. Grafs are another beast, where apple juice and beer wort are fermented together. Add into this the native microflora from wild yeasts and bacteria, as Tom and Jonny have done with Foxbic, and you're in for quite a ride.

Foxwhelp is a magical, sharp apple, tangy and aromatic from bud to bottle. Three barrels were filled with different proportions of Foxwhelp juice and turbid wort (see life story, right) and left in peace to ferment together for 10 months.

After fermentation was finished, the barrels were tasted and reblended before bottling. Eight months later the Foxbic emerged, as if from a chrysalis.

'We weren't sure what to expect,' says Jonny. He needn't have worried.

It pours lemon/lightest peach in colour, with lemony notes alongside very fine bubbles. The acidity of a lambic beer integrates well with unmistakable apple notes. There's a light Belgian texture with a tangy seam running through. The flavours evolve on swirling – and ageing – with the lemony/tangerine pure flavours becoming more savoury and herbal.

While Batch #1 is long gone, its second incarnation is due, nature permitting, in 2019. Best set your alarm.

region: Herefordshire/ Gloucestershire, England

fruits: a blend of cider apple, Foxwhelp, with lambic wort

life story: barrels of Foxwhelp juice blended with turbid wort, prepared to ensure the best mix of carbohydrates and sugars for a mixed culture fermentation; blending, bottling, further ageing before release

abv: 4.7%

if you like this: try Oliver's/Brooklyn/ Thornbridge, The Serpent. Due out 2019: Foxbic #2; Big Red, Dabinett/ red ale blend

experience: Cider Salon, June; visit Oliver's Ciderhouse, Saturday; visits to Mills Brewing welcome by appointment

oliversciderandperry.co.uk

millsbrewing.wordpress.com

LITTLE POMONA
ART OF DARKNESS, 2015

region: Herefordshire, England

fruit: mainly bittersweet Ellis Bitter, a splash of fellow bittersweet Harry Masters Jersey and a little Foxwhelp, one of the oldest surviving cider varieties

life story: Ellis Bitter undergoes natural yeast fermentation; left on lees for a year, aged in neutral, ex-whisky barrels for a year; topped up with HMJ and Foxwhelp; six months in bottle

abv: 7%

if you like this: try Little Pomona's Old Man & The Bee, still; The Rainbow, traditional method, sparkling

experience: Cider Salon, June; follow social media for events and tastings news

littlepomona.com

Imagine you're heading out into an autumnal day. There's a mist out there, you're rustling through the forest, you kick the leaves. There are the aromas of ripe, russet-hued apples. Warm peaches. Hints of sandalwood. That's our cider, the Art of Darkness. So called because it's emerging into the light after a lengthy spell in the dark, including a year in beautiful ex-whisky barrels.

The palate is layered, with dusky tannins. Dry in sweetness terms but with fine fruit notes, there are flavours of ripe, yellow apples, of thick-cut marmalade, of fresh tart peaches. Like a freshly sharpened pencil, the acids from our friend the vibrant Foxwhelp apple sketch out the experience. That's the effect of time. Just apples and time: our mantra at Little Pomona, the cidery my husband James and I set up in 2014.

So how did we get here? James and I became entranced with the complexity offered by the apples in Herefordshire when we visited one summer. On our return home, the beguiling tastes and the friendly welcome of the cidermaking community proved irresistible.

Two years of searching, then, just as we were about to give up, our little orchard appeared. With its gentle, south-facing slope, Little Pomona had found a home. Friends and family gave generously of their time and thoughts. Our friend and mentor Tom Oliver guided us, helping us to see that the apple knows its own mind. It's ready when it's ready...

Much like the Art of Darkness, the last cider from our first commercial harvest. The tannins have softened and the layers have emerged. It's a discussion to be had. We hope you'll be part of it.

• Dry Still Cider •
Little Pomona
ART OF DARKNESS
Alc 7% Vol
2015
50 cle

DRAGON ORCHARD CIDER
2016
PUTLEY GOLD
HEREFORDSHIRE CIDER PGI
ESTATE GROWN & BOTTLED

ONCE UPON A TREE
PUTLEY GOLD, 2016

Simon Day's Eureka moment was The Big Apple's annual Blossomtime Festival in Putley, a Herefordshire cider and perry heartland. As well as meeting the makers at the legendary Putley Trials, Simon, an experienced winemaker himself, heard a scientific talk from leading cidermaking authority Andrew Lea.

'I thought "It really is winemaking!"' he says. 'All those different flavours.' Inspired, Simon wanted to create something, but something different.

While working in Jersey a few years earlier, he used to hop across the Channel to St-Malo for Sunday lunch. 'You'd have a fantastic bottle of local cider,' he says. 'It was a drink that went well with the local food.' That was what was missing in the UK.

But he had no fruit. Luckily, living in Putley, Simon was in the right area. He used to walk his dog past Dragon Orchard, the beautiful 9-ha (22-acre) orchard farmed by pioneering cropsharers Norman and Ann Stanier. There was a meeting of minds and, together, Simon and his wife Hannah and the Staniers created Once Upon A Tree.

Simon crafts his ciders with a style of food in mind. The Putley Gold in my glass is destined for classic dishes like roast pork, while the less tannic Marcle Ridge is aimed more at fish. Clear gold in colour, Putley Gold shows very ripe apple and pear flavours, with peaches and apricots thrown in, plus fine tannins and balancing acids.

Simon recalls his first glimpse of the sparkling elegance of the 18th-century glassware in Hereford Cider Museum. '"This really was the wine of England in the 17th and 18th century," I thought.' With his input, it's regaining its place.

region: Herefordshire, England

fruit: a blend of bittersweet Dabinett and Ellis Bitter, with sharp Brown's Apple for acid and fragrance

life story: apples are harvested often late in the season to ensure proper ripeness – 'one of the secrets' – and fermented separately, before blending

abv: 7%

if you like this: try Chapel Pleck Sparkling Perry; Blenheim Superb Ice Cider; Wild Flight, part of profits go towards International Centre for Birds of Prey

experience: Blossomtime and Harvestime Festivals, The Big Apple, Herefordshire; tours, tasting, Friday–Saturday, September; check Facebook for events

onceuponatree.co.uk

GREGG'S PIT
BARNET, BRANDY & WINNALS LONGDON

region: Herefordshire, England

fruit: Barnet, Brandy, Winnals Longdon perry pears

life story: sourced locally, pressed on an ancient stone press, six month fermentation before bottling and bottle conditioning

abv: 6%

if you like this: match with fish and herb-infused dishes; try Thorn Champagne Method perry, also Aylton Red, Blakeney Red, Gregg's Pit 'house blend'

experience: throughout the year, the monthly Kempley Produce Market; Cider Salon, June; The Big Apple Harvestime festival, Herefordshire, with a 'walk, talk and taste' wander through the orchards; available in Italy, The Netherlands, Sweden, Columbia

greggs-pit.co.uk

'We put this trio together for the first time in 2009 by happenstance,' says James Marsden, one half of the duo behind Gregg's Pit, explaining how he and partner Helen Woodman had been offered the chance to harvest the fruit from an orchard near Ross-on-Wye. By then, Gregg's Pit had won the Champion Perry award at the local Big Apple Blossomtime trials 10 times, no mean feat considering how much of a challenge the coquettish perry pear is.

Gregg's Pit itself is an inspiringly evocative set-up in the Herefordshire cider heartland of Much Marcle. Within sight of May Hill, the all-important touchpoint for those growing perry pears, James and Helen have two orchards, one with standard trees, the other wilder, dominated by a few vast, ancient perry pear trees.

While Barnet is in fairly good supply, Brandy and Winnals Longdon are relatively rare. Each brings something different to the blend, with Brandy offering colour and rich, almost woody aromatics, and Winnals Longdon good acids and wonderful floral and fruity fragrance. 'It's always a tricky judgement call when to harvest,' says James. As it turns out, this is the blend which visitors often see being pressed during The Big Apple Harvestime festival.

Pale yellow in the glass with a gentle sparkle, this is fragrant and delicate on the nose, reminding me of a Victorian cottage garden, with elderflowers, chamomile, plus pears and pear blossom, and an underlying hint of starfruit. Soft and rounded in the mouth, the medium-bodied texture is enlivened by subtle richness and balancing acidity.

'We are the *garagistes* of cidermakers,' says James. Long may that continue.

Gregg's Pit
HEREFORDSHIRE PERRY

ROSS · ON · WYE
Whole Juice
Moorcroft & Bartestree Squash
Moorcroft, a popular Worcestershire Pear from the Malvern Hills, combined with a Herefordshire variety, Bartestree Squash, producing a balanced full flavour perry.

ROSS-ON-WYE CIDER & PERRY
MOORCROFT & BARTESTREE SQUASH, 2016

There are literally dozens of different perries on sale in Ross-on-Wye Cider & Perry Co's wood cabin of a shop behind The Yew Tree pub in Peterstow, just across the orchards from the cidery at Broome Farm. Founder Mike Johnson is one of those producers who can coax something wonderful out of these precocious pears, a legacy which son Albert is ably continuing with.

A few decades ago, when Mike was planting up parts of Broome Farm with mainstream varieties for sale to Bulmers, ever the orchard explorer he'd be sneaking in a few extra trees of something interesting. So alongside the 120 cider-apple varieties, you can find 30 different perry pears too. Thus, even with the famous difficulties surrounding the harvesting of perry pears – 'pears do turn over so quickly,' says Albert – you can see why it was a difficult decision which perry to choose.

Much deliberation later, the Moorcroft & Bartestree Squash blend won. It's got fragrance, it's got style. It's understated but it has character. Pale gold in the glass, there's a wonderful elegance of aromatics; the flowers carry all the way through, alongside some green notes, white melon and a touch of starfruit-skin-type waxiness, and a mango-skin fragrance on the finish. Medium bodied, it's perfect solo, or a treat with white fish and light meats simply cooked with herbs; or a goat's cheese salad or tartlet.

Moorcroft is highly regarded as a perry pear, although it can be temperamental. 'And they rot so quickly. We have to hand-pick them every two days,' says Albert. Bartestree, on the other hand, is pretty rare but 'extremely reliable', he says. 'Intense, tempting pear aromas. It's impossible to smell and not want to immediately sip.' I agree.

region: Herefordshire, England

fruit: Moorcroft, a Worcestershire perry pear, Bartestree Squash, a Herefordshire perry pear

life story: harvested from Broome Farm orchards; long, cool fermentation

abv: 7%

if you like this: try Bartestree Squash, Yellow Huffcap, Gin Pear single varietals; visit the shop for many, many more

experience: orchard tours and tasting; The Yew Tree Inn in Peterstow, the peerless Ross Cider Shop; camping; monthly Cider Club; the legendary Ross Cider Festival in late August

rosscider.com

DUNKERTONS
BLACK FOX

region: Herefordshire, England

fruit: a 10-strong blend, including the classics Kingston Black and Dabinett, but also the fragrant Court Royal, the scented gem Stoke Red and, coincidentally, Dunkerton Late, raised by a Glastonbury-based gentleman of the same name

life story: harvest whenever each variety is ripe; slow fermentation in stainless steel before racking and bottling

abv: 7%

if you like this: try Breakwells Seedling; Browns; Organic Perry

experience: visit shop in Pembridge, Thursday–Friday; visit Tasting Room at Dowdeswell Park, Cheltenham; follow Facebook for events

dunkertonscider.co.uk

We'd never seen anything like it. A beautifully curated orchard where the trees were named and known individually. There was even a plaque describing who was responsible and when the planting took place. This was back in 2011, and we were with Susie and Ivor Dunkerton, researching for my tourism website.

Having decided to escape their London lives, Susie and Ivor founded Dunkertons in 1980. Both careful and caring, a few years later they began planting their own trees, beginning with that prize bittersharp Kingston Black, alongside stalwart bittersweet Dabinett, and another they became renowned for, the aromatic, bittersharp Breakwells Seedling – I can see a bottle on my shelf now.

Organic status came soon after, as did a small number of partner orchardists. Finally, the Dunkertons' own perry orchard, with 12 varieties and over 150 trees, completed the picture.

One of my favourites from the start, Black Fox continues to be a skilful blend of 10 apple varieties. Named after the elusive local legend – well you never see a black fox, do you? – this is off-dry and dark gold in the glass, with layers of broad, baked apple and thick-cut marmalade flavours, a balanced tang, and tannins that want to be noticed.

In 2014, Susie and Ivor handed over the baton to their son, Julian, who teamed up with long-time friend Jeremy 'Bean' Benson. Recently stepping back from trendy clothing brand Superdry which he founded, Julian has moved production an hour's journey east, to Dowdeswell Park in Cheltenham. Ivor passed away in 2016, but Susie remains involved, and the heart of the fruit, one key quality, remains in Pembridge. A legacy to be proud of.

Alc 7% vol
500ml
Black Fox
cider
DUNKERTONS

Pilton
TAMOSHANTA
barrel-fermented
Somerset keeved cider
75cl

PILTON CIDER
TAMOSHANTA, 2016

Glastonbury is often thought to be a place with mystical powers, so perhaps it's appropriate that one of England's leading exponents of the magical keeving process is based in, and named after, the tiny neighbouring village of Pilton.

A home cidermaker for a number of years, when Martin Berkeley and his wife Angela moved to Shepton Mallet they noticed orchard fruit going to waste and determined to do something with it. Having been brought up in France, Angela favoured the French style of cider, relying on keeving to leave a rustic, residual sweetness. With Angela's help, Martin learnt the ropes in France – there are no keeving classes in the UK – and now you'll find Pilton all around Britain, plus the USA, Spain and Italy.

Sourcing his fruit locally, another bit of magic Martin has access to is 88 Somerset cider-apple varieties in the library orchard behind the historic Shepton Mallett cider mill.

Martin adds these to his blends, and Tamoshanta takes Martin's original Pilton cider one step further. Each Burns Night at the end of January, cider is filled into ex-Speyside whisky barrels to finish its fermentation before bottling. The cider is named in honour of *Tam o' Shanter*, one of the epic poems from Scots literary legend, Rabbie Burns.

Beautiful, warm, sun-kissed apple aromas with yellow apples and hints of demerara sugar hit first on the nose. With an elegant sparkle of tiny bubbles, the barrel comes through on the palate, giving the tannins a drying effect. The warm apple and peach sweetness on the palate is balanced with acidity and gentle to moderate tannins. Enchanting.

region: Somerset, England

fruit: orchard blends of bittersweet and bittersharp apples from Somerset

life story: keeved and fermented in the autumn, filled into ex-Scotch whisky barrels on Burns Night to finish fermentation, before final conditioning in the bottle

abv: 4.7%

if you like this: try Pilton original, Ice & Fire ciders

experience: Cider Salon, June; check out Events tab on Pilton website; cidermakers enjoy Martin's hospitality every year with his friendly Cidermakers Bottle-Share during the Royal Bath & West Show, May/June

pilton.com

PERRY'S
TREMLETT, COLLECTORS CARD NO 4

region: Somerset, England

fruit: Tremlett's Bitter, primarily from their Knowle St Giles orchard

life story: harvested in October, fermented with a mix of wild and cultured yeasts in stainless steel, and bottled fairly early

abv: 5.9%

if you like this: try Premium Vintage; Somerset Redstreak; Puffin, bottle conditioned

experience: visit Cider Farm; Tea Room and Eatery (Monday–Saturday); visit and taste in Farm Shop; visit vintage museum in 16th-century thatched cider barn, with equipment; pop-up yoga followed by cake in the cider garden

perryscider.co.uk

It's nearly a century since William Churchill began making cider in Dowlish Wake, midway between the market towns of Ilminster and Crewkerne in Somerset. Back then it was only a sideline to his blacksmithing, but he obviously had the knack because the business lived on, passing to his nephews, Henry and Bert Perry. Today it's Henry's grandson George running the show, with dad John still very much in the picture.

While other cidermakers were bought or bailed out, the Perrys kept carving out their niche: artisanal ciders. The aim is to 'really champion the complexity and full apple characteristics of full juice ciders', George tells me. Recent plantings took their orchards to 14ha (35 acres), and they are well known for their single varietals. This prowess comes partly because they tend to press apples and ferment the juice by individual variety.

I've chosen Tremlett because it's such a dramatic character. Generally it's regarded as too bitter to be a single varietal. It's also biennial, slow to ferment, and not easy to grow. But it works well for George and his cidermaker Gavyn Luck, and it's been one of their Single-Varietal series for six years.

And this works. A smoky note on the nose warns of danger, the tannins are persistent but fine and subtle, the balance is beautiful. Medium dry, there's a good complexity of apricots as well as ripe apple flavours – think Russet and Cox's Orange Pippin. And it's stylishly packaged, adorned with a Water Boatman image, one of the Collectors Card labels designed by Wales-based illustrator and printmaker Tom Frost, aka The Boy Frost.

I think we're all happy William gave up the blacksmithing.

PERRY'S
SOMERSET CIDER
COLLECTORS CARD Nº04
SINGLE VARIETY CIDER
TREMLETT

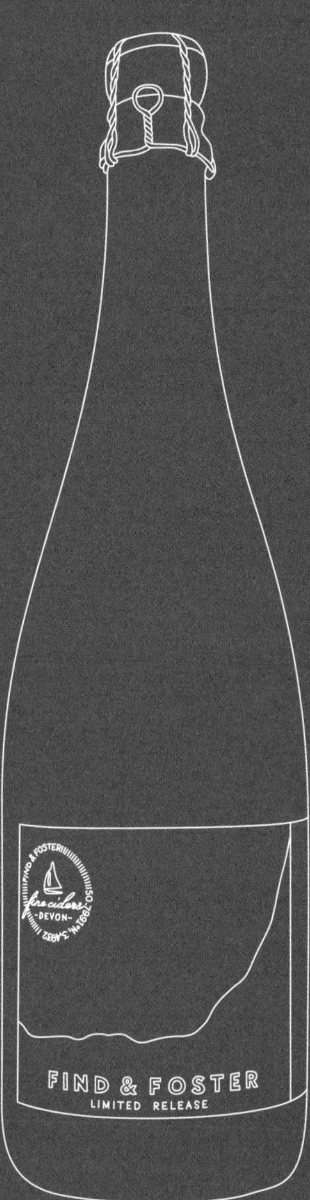
FIND & FOSTER
fine ciders
DEVON
FIND & FOSTER
LIMITED RELEASE

FIND & FOSTER
MÉTHODE TRADITIONELLE, 2015

'We saw an owl there today! There's lots of evidence of them. Lots of woodpecker holes, too. There's so much dead wood from the trees that haven't survived.'

This is Polly Hilton, founder and cidermaker at Find & Foster, talking about the richness of wildlife she finds in the orchards she tends. Incredulous when she heard that 90% of the trees in her native Devon had been grubbed up since World War II, Polly got in touch with the farmers. In exchange for looking after the trees, could she turn the fruit into cider, thus making the orchards financially sustainable once more? The response was enthusiastic. Now there are five she tends, with more waiting in line.

'The apples are so beautiful and so different,' she says. 'Every single taste that you could imagine. And a lot of the varieties in the orchards I look after I don't know what they are. One of the apples looks exactly like a rhubarb and custard sweet. Strange, don't you find, how sometimes they taste like they look?' she says. 'This one is really small, perfectly spherical.'

This affinity with the orchard's bounty comes through in her ciders.

Her first *méthode traditionelle* cider is glorious. A beautiful nose with Russet and soft, fuzzy peach notes, warm Cox and a hint of Braeburn. The persistent bead of bubbles is mesmerising. Great balance on the palate, with a cleansing acidity alongside ripe red and yellow apple notes, and a beautifully long finish.

Polly's sole aim is to let the apples express themselves. With her care and love, I'd say that's assured.

region: Devon, England

fruit: bittersweet/bittersharp blend from traditional orchards, including several unknown varieties and one of Polly's favourites, the Devonshire Buckland

life story: harvest happens tree by tree, when each is perfectly ripe; seven month secondary fermentation with further ageing after disgorging before release for more complexity

abv: 8%

if you like this: look for Polly's keeved ciders, and when the apples suggest it, her special blends

experience: follow Polly's journey on Instagram; tune into Fine Cider (thefinecider.company) who distribute her; head to Darts Farm in Topsham

findandfosterfineciders.com

SANDFORD ORCHARDS
SAINT LOUIS DRY HOPPED

region: Devon, England

fruit: bittersharp-heavy blend of Devon cider apples; whole leaf Ella and Willamette hops

life story: slow, cool, natural yeast fermentation of around one month; six months to mature; dry hopping at blending; lightly sweetened and carbonated

abv: 5.5%

if you like this: try the small batch Fine Cider range; Old Kirton on draught, pressed the really old-fashioned way, through straw

experience: visit The Cider Works shop, take a tour, visit the Tap Room bar on a Friday evening; join the Secret Cider Society for special food pairing evenings

sandfordorchards.co.uk

They say chance favours the prepared. The day after Dan Kopman, US craft brewer of note – 25 years at the helm of Saint Louis' Schlafly brewery – visited Barny Butterfield's Sandford Orchards in rural Devon ('he came for the scrumpy, stayed for the meal,' says Barny with a smile), they found themselves on the same train on the way back to London. 'We got on and got chatting,' says Barny. It's a fair journey from Devon. The result? Saint Louis Dry Hopped.

While Barny describes Dan as 'the godfather of craft beer', he is no slouch himself. The founder of a burgeoning craft cidery with a sizeable list of authentic ciders and a talented roster of staff, Barny has drive and vision, and loves experimenting.

The 16-month gestation period saw Barny spend a week over at Schlafly, mucking in and clearing out the mash tuns while he found out more about the intricacies of hops. Hop a cider too heavily and it's a confected, clumsy affair. 'Hops are just flowers, and how they exhibit depends not just on what they are and their quality but how the hopping is done,' says Barny. Perfect the technique with Barny's 'wonderful bittersweet fruit', and you arrive with the distinctive character that is Saint Louis Dry Hopped.

Floral and citrusy aromas lead to a balanced, mellow, light-bodied palate. The hopping is subtle – neither wanted a mini-me IPA – while the palate is fresh, with fruit acids fighting off any cloying tendencies. The hop oils add a touch of astringency, while a floral fragrance from the hop flowers sings through on the close.

SANDFORD ORCHARDS
SCHLAFLY
SAINT LOUIS
5.5%
DRY HOPPED
DEVON CIDER
WITH U.S. HOPS
SERIES 03

LANCOMBE
RISING
5% ABV
75cl ℮
NATURALLY SPARKLING CIDER

WEST MILTON CIDER CO
LANCOMBE RISING

The Royal Bath & West Show owes its 2017 Supreme Champion to a string of horses. Back in 2000, Dawn Poole's horse Spocky and the children's ponies, Bunty and Popper, were sharing their paddock with a raft of old cider-apple trees. Dawn and her husband Nick realised that, for the horses' health, they needed to gather in the apples at harvest-time. One thing led to another, and soon not only were they making their own cider, they'd set up the West Milton Cider Club for fellow home cidermakers.

'Thus began a fascinating voyage into the folklore, the processes and alchemy of the cidermaker's art,' Nick says.

Along with joining up with pomological doyenne Liz Copas to hunt down Dorset's lost apple varieties, Nick established Powerstock, the county's leading cider festival, and an event credited with triggering the renaissance in the county's cidermaking. Nick and Dawn also became fascinated with keeving, the technique whereby some natural sweetness stays in the cider. 'This involved many visits to Normandy to learn the old processes,' says Nick, who admits to 'lots of experimentation' before being happy with his own keeved cider, the champion Lancombe Rising.

Amber in the glass, this has great apple sweetness on the palate – think rich Russet combined with Cox's Orange Pippin, plus plenty of baked apple aromas. On the nose, it's an autumnal bouquet, with warm apple, hazelnuts, a hint of herbs and a touch of light caramel. Tannins are dusky, enjoyable and very food friendly.

Thinking back to that paddock-cum-orchard at the turn of the century, perhaps it's horses who are a man's best friend.

region: Dorset, England

fruit: a blend, over three-quarters bittersweets, including Dabinett, Chisel Jersey, Browns and Michelin; to ensure maximum ripeness, the fruit is collected after it falls

life story: the juice undergoes the keeving process before a three-month, cool fermentation, bottling with some residual yeast, and three months of further maturation before release

abv: 5%

if you like this: try Dorset Twilight, dry, still; Dorset Moonlight, medium, lightly carbonated

experience: check website and social media; head to Melplash Cider Festival, the reincarnated Powerstock, July

westmiltoncider.co.uk

DORSET NECTAR
TOP O' THE HILL

region: Dorset, England

fruit: a blend of bittersharps: Browns, Porter's Perfection; sweet: Sweet Coppin; bittersweet: Dabinett, Harry Masters Jersey, Michelin

life story: a blend from 2016 and 2015; while the 2016 was fermenting with natural yeasts, a third-by-volume of 2015 was blended in, to achieve consistency

abv: 5%

if you like this: try Old Harry Rocks Dry Vintage Cider; Elderflower Cider

experience: visit Cider Tap Room & Shop, open all year; Tours & Tasting: Thursday, Friday and Saturday; head to Melplash Cider Festival (formerly Powerstock), July

dorsetnectar.co.uk

Dorset may not have as noisy a profile in the cider world as Somerset or the Three Counties, but its cidermaking heritage stretches back centuries. In recent decades, however, what fruit there is has generally been under contract to the big guys.

That's changing, and producers like Dorset Nectar are leading the charge. A family business, Oliver and Penny Strong set up Dorset Nectar in the mid-2000s. A noted sculptor, he needed more space and happened upon a barn along with 3,000 trees under contract. When the Strongs were refused the option of keeping some fruit, they took the plunge, terminated the contract and set up on their own.

Ten years later the family picked up Champion Organic Trophy at the Royal Bath & West Show with this cider, Top O' The Hill.

Resolutely dry and a warming amber in colour, aromas of apples and apricots kick matters off, while delicious, mouthcoating tannins continue the experience. The sparkle accentuates an inspiring balance between freshness and warm, ripe apple notes.

Of the six-apple blend, for son Ryan – he's looking after cidermaking these days with Oliver – Porter's Perfection is the star, not least because of its role in Dorset Nectar's early days.

Notoriously late to harvest, by the time Porter's Perfection was ready the year the Strongs began, the mill it was destined for had already closed. 'Having not made cider before, with just a few books and some very helpful advice from Cider by Rosie's Rose Grant, we made our first cider. We took it to the Royal Bath & West Show and won an award for it.'

They haven't looked back.

DORSET NECTAR
• BRIDPORT •
DORSET CIDER
TOP O' THE HILL
An artisan cider with a natural sparkle, Medium/Dry.
- 500ml - ORGANIC - 5% ABV -

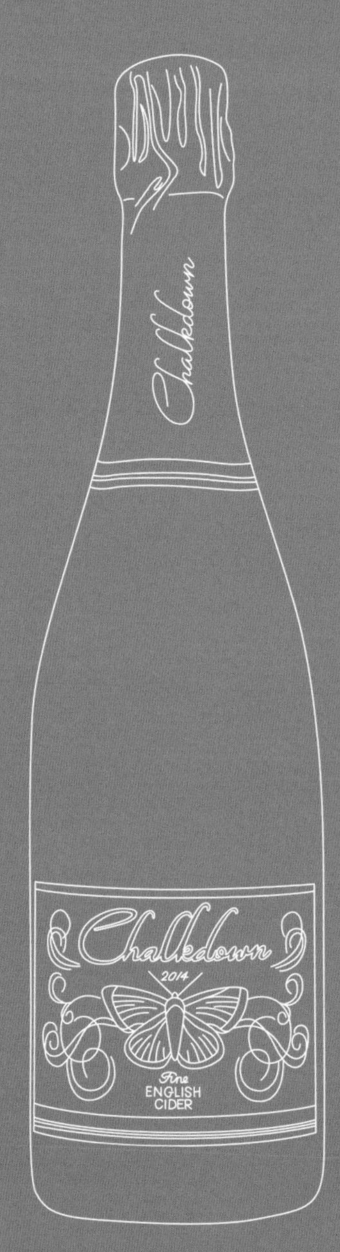
Chalkdown
Chalkdown
2014
Fine
ENGLISH
CIDER

BRIGHT & FRESH

CHALKDOWN CIDER 2014

Chalkdown Cider happened almost by accident. Having graduated from wine school – Plumpton College in Sussex – Piotr Nahajski headed to the Champagne region on a study visit. On his return, he happened to try Gospel Green, then being made by founders James and Cathy Lane, in Sussex. Made using the traditional method with dessert apples, Gospel Green showed Piotr possibilities beyond the West Country style.

This got Piotr thinking. What could he create which would marry lighter-toned, dessert fruit with the effervescence of sparkling wine? And would this benefit from ageing on the lees before release? Chalkdown is the answer, and yes, 18 months' ageing does add layers of complexity.

Piotr teamed up with Will Dobson at Hill Farm Orchards on the Hampshire Downs. Piotr knew the sorts of apples he wanted to create the base blend for his traditional-method cider, and through tasting and analysis he homed in on his blend.

It's a mix primarily of Cox's Orange Pippin and Egremont Russet, plus a handful of other dessert apples, including the perfumed Kanzi – 'it's like rose petals.'

Pale lemony gold in the glass, this has a glorious persistent sparkle. Fragrant notes of tangerine zest and warm apples give way to ripe baked apples on the palate. Light and crisp, the high acidity and tingly sparkle give a very fresh, mouthwatering finish.

The cider is named after the Chalkhill Blue butterfly, a well-known resident of the Hampshire Downs. Hampshire may still only be home to a clutch of cider producers, but those who are there are beginning to make their presence felt.

region: Hampshire, England

fruit: a dessert apple blend, mainly zingy Cox's Orange Pippin, honeyed Egrement Russet with its almost nutty character, plus Bramley, Kanzi, Braeburn

life story: hand-picked apples, light pressing; fermented in steel tanks, aged for six months on lees in tanks; secondary bottle fermentation; 18 months in bottle before disgorging and *dosage*; bottling, three months before release

abv: 8.3%

if you like this: try Gospel Green Cyder; Aspall 1728; Find & Foster

experience: check out Facebook for news of events and festivals

chalkdowncider.com

KENTISH PIP
WILD SUMMER, ELDERFLOWER CIDER

region: Kent, England

fruit: fragrant Katy apple, plus Greensleeves – normally a pollinator, but left to go really ripe, it gives spice and acidity too

life story: fermentation continues until the spring; once complete, elderflower cordial is added prior to a light carbonation and canning

abv: 4%

if you like this: try Skylark, Apple Cider, Kentish Pip's first sparkler; Forager, Hedgerow Berry Cider, inspired by mum Rosie's hedgerow jelly; Vintage Pip, dessert/cider apple blend

experience: visit Woolton Farm shop, Monday–Friday; Blues on the Farm, June; Canterbury Food & Drink Festival, September; follow social media

kentishpip.co.uk

Sam Mount illustrates the modern face of Kentish cider. He blends creative organisational skills (he used to produce music festivals) with an innate curiosity about flavours – when he was young, his mum Rosie had him out foraging for all manner of berries and fruits – along with what he's absorbed from his father, Mark, on the cidermaking front.

The Mounts are in Kent, within striking distance of the historic city of Canterbury. An apple stronghold, their orchards predominantly host dessert varieties, with favourites such as Cox, Discovery and Russet. Russet's texture and thick skin 'give it a bit more depth', says Sam. 'It speaks of where it comes from.'

A long-time home cidermaker – most apple farmers were – Mark began Kentish Pip in 2012. Sam is one of many to graduate from Peter Mitchell's Cider & Perry Academy in Gloucestershire, and is decidedly outward-looking. 'There's a great scene in New Zealand,' he says, while admitting to having Latvian and Breton ciders in his fridge as we speak.

I've chosen the elderflower-imbued Wild Summer. Elderflowers are collected in late May. Since rain washes the pollen out, the Mounts hope for a sunny day. Making the most of whole heads of flowers, they give the little branches a small shake. Then it's time to create the cordial, with water, lemon zest and sugar.

Watery white in the glass, Wild Summer is beautifully fragrant, medium to sweet in nature, with just enough acidity to balance. Pollen and nectar notes are interwoven with ripe dessert-apple flavours, while the sparkle lends a nice palate-cleansing note, preventing the cider from becoming cloying in any way. Contemporary yet traditional, much like Sam's approach.

KENTISH
PiP
WILD
SUMMER
SPARKLING
Elderflower
cider

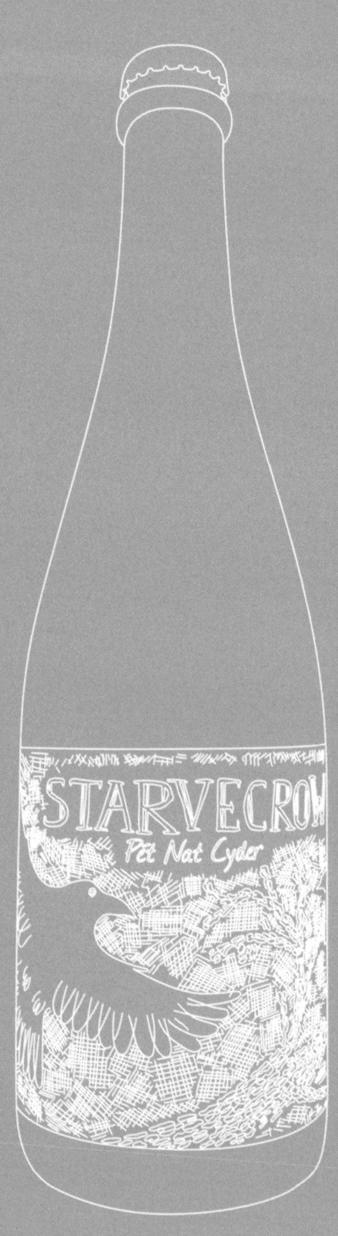
STARVECROW
Pét Nat Cyder

STARVECROW
PÉT NAT CYDER, 2017

'I wanted to do a small amount of red wine with my small *qvevri*. And I didn't have the grapes there at the right time, so I filled it with cider – and it's absolutely delicious!' This is Ben Walgate of Starvecrow, the cidery he founded with neighbouring farmer Steve Reeve, explaining how he came to be among the first to create cider in *qvevri*, the fermenting vessel favoured by the ancient Georgians.

'It's Steve's apples, so I thought, just go for it!' he continues. '*Qvevri* – they have this weird way of taking care of themselves. They have this clarity to them. It's really inspiring.'

While Ben is a newbie to cider, he's been involved in the wine industry for over a decade. Formerly CEO at dynamic Kent wine estate Gusbourne, now he's following his own biodynamic path with Tillingham Wines.

Meanwhile, Steve's family has been in apples for generations. They have 26ha (65 acres) of trees, the average age of which is over 35 years, all culinary/dessert – we are on the Sussex/Kent borders.

We have their *pét nat* here, fermented not in *qvevri* but in oak barrels.

Pale lemon in colour, it is as fresh as spring, with elegant apricot notes on the palate alongside grapefruit and lemon zest. It's high in acids, lightly cloudy, with green apple notes of Bramley adding a touch of contrast and a lengthy citrus-tinged finish.

For Ben, the goal is to express *terroir*. 'That's always been my interest. I have this fascination. There's this quality that wine perhaps more than any [other] alcoholic beverage has: a sense of place. It might be that cider does too, and I think it probably does. I just haven't got there.' Don't think it will take him long.

region: East Sussex, England

fruit: a south-east culinary/dessert blend of snappy Bramley, scented Golden Delicious, sweet yet tangy Jonagold, rich Braeburn

life story: juice blend from four varieties co-fermented in barrel; bottled while still some residual sugar to finish fermenting; disgorged and topped up with the same cider

abv: 5.5%

if you like this: try Natural Cider, Qvevri Cider, Bourbon Cider

experience: Cider Salon, June; follow Instagram

HAWKES
SOUL TRADER, 2017

region: Kent/ London, England

fruit: the dessert apple, Discovery, from fourth generation orchardist Robert Hinge in Kent

life story: apples kept for one month for full ripeness before milling; month long, temperature-controlled fermentation; aged on lees for a month; light carbonation

abv: 5.4%

if you like this: try Urban Orchard; others in Single Variety series; the Graff collaborations

experience: head to the Tap Room; check out tours and masterclasses: Cider Making, Cider and Cheese Pairing

wearehawkes.com

In Britain, there are not many urban cideries, and even fewer urban cidery tap rooms. So the news of Hawkes opening its place in London was welcome indeed. Inspired by his American travels, Simon Wright, founder of Hawkes, has boldly set up shop in a railway arch, slap bang in the middle of the so-called Bermondsey Beer Mile. Less than a year in, they've expanded into arches either side and announced big investment from BrewDog, so signs are that they've really caught the wave.

Head past the tap wall and pizza oven to find the undoubted star of this gaff: the cider house. There's an apple store, mill and press, plus gleaming floor-to-ceiling tanks. And more often than not, former winemaker-turned-cidermaker, Roberto Basilico, happy to share what's going on as he crafts Hawkes' ciders.

Hawkes began, and continues, with Urban Orchard cider, created with a mix of culinary apples plus up to a third donated apples during harvest-time – 3kg (6½lb) scores you a bottle in exchange.

From 2017, Roberto has also been producing smaller batches, such as this, Hawkes' first single-varietal cider, Soul Trader. Almost water-white and very fragrant, it captures well the scented nature of the Discovery apple. A cross between Worcester Pearmain, the popular, often strawberry-scented variety, and the less well-known Beauty of Bath from Victorian times, Discovery is popular – and successful – in cidermaking circles. Soul Trader's light sparkle, clean apple- and pear-tinged flavours, balanced acids and hint of lime on the finish show why.

Simon believes that cider is misunderstood and, as well as giving back to the community (he's got previous on that), education is part of the mission. Good idea.

BORN & RAISED

HAWKES

— LONDON —

SOUL TRADER

CIDER PRESSED IN LONDON

ALC. 5.4% VOL.

ASPALL
1728
FINE SPARKLING CYDER
2015
VINTAGE
ALC.
11%
VOL

ASPALL
1728, 2015

Back in 1728, Clement Chevallier landed in Suffolk from his native Jersey. Aged just 31, within days he was planting apple trees he'd brought with him on the voyage. Swiftly dispelling his critics' qualms about the sustainability of a cidermaking business, Clement lit the touchpaper for a cidermaking zeal that has lasted eight generations.

Today Aspall's orchards contain 46 different varieties. Henry Chevallier-Guild, who with his brother, Barry, currently head up the firm, admits to a soft spot for the tart, sharp varieties, in particular Bramley's Seedling. It's this apple that's at the heart of 1728, the champagne-method cider crafted for Aspall by its head cidermaker Colin Valentine. 'We wanted to enable the raciness to get through,' says Henry.

Inspired by the *champenois*, Henry insists on the 1728 being given 18 months on its lees after its secondary fermentation. Henry is also proud to point out that it was glassmakers in the Forest of Dean who developed the stronger glass that became essential to the Champagne industry, glass that could withstand the extra pressures caused by secondary fermentation.

So pick up a wine glass, pour a decent measure, swirl and sniff. Pale yellow in colour, citrus and savoury hints mix together on the nose, leading to an elegant palate with those savoury notes to the fore. Tiny bubbles are lively and long lasting. There are marmalade and tangerine notes underneath. Perfect as an aperitif, it's ideal with sushi, shellfish and mushroom risotto. Very elegant and definitely east coast (of England) in style, due to its imperceptible tannins, I reckon Clement would have made a return trip to Jersey just to share 1728 with those he left behind.

region: Suffolk, England

fruit: Bramley apples from two English strongholds – Kent, and Wisbech in Suffolk – plus around 10% bittersweet blend

life story: following initial fermentation, champagne yeast is added for the secondary bottle fermentation; cider stays on its lees for 18 months before disgorging

abv: 11%

if you like this: try Premier Cru; Imperial Vintage; Perronelle's Blush

experience: check website for events, including Suffolk Show, May; Jimmy's Festival, Ipswich, July; Aldeburgh Food & Drink Festival, September; Tennis Classic at Hurlingham, June

aspall.co.uk

HALLETS
REAL CIDER

region: Caerphilly, South Wales

fruit: Dabinett plus a blend of sweet/bittersweet/ bittersharp/sharp cider varieties

life story: the apples are milled, then macerated for a day to help flavours and colour, and to assist with the keeving process

abv: 6%

if you like this: try Hallets in can; track down on draught: Heartbreaker, the original dry Blaengawney cider that won the Pewterers' Trophy; Oak Aged

experience: stay at Blaengawney Farm; Hallets Bonfire Festival, November; follow Facebook and Instagram for event news; check out digital stories on Welsh Perry & Cider Society website

halletsrealcider.co.uk

Can't be a bad sign, winning the highly coveted Pewterers' Trophy for Champion British Farmhouse Cider at the Royal Bath & West Show before you're fully commercial.

While Andy Hallett had been making cider for a while, albeit as a hobby, this helped trigger the next stage: setting up Hallets Real Cider with his wife, Annie. Son Andrew has recently joined the crew, taking over cidermaking, among other duties.

The Bath & West win back in 2008 was for the Hallett's Blaengawny Cider, named after the farm where they are still based. Located 300m (1,000ft) up on the spur of a valley in South Wales within sight of Mynydd Maen. Where mining used to hold sway, now nature has reclaimed its territory and you're more likely to see mountain bikers than miners.

Rebranded as Hallets in 2009, today they have 1,200 trees, including the largest single planting of Frederick, the previously endangered Monmouthshire variety. Although still young, these trees are already contributing to Real Cider.

Andy likens cidermaking to painting. Just as an artist has a colour palette to work with, so apples provide the flavour palate with which a cidermaker crafts his or her cider.

For each batch of Real Cider, Andy takes Dabinett from the previous year, and blends it with an artful selection from the current harvest. This might include classic cider varieties like Harry Masters Jersey and Brown's, with its 'lovely sherbety feel'.

The result? A full-bodied cider, golden in colour with distinctive yet approachable tannins. Rich notes of baked apple mingle with spice, the sparkle is restrained and the finish is moreish and memorable. Much like their Bath & West win, I'd wager.

TRADITIONALLY
MADE
HALLETS
REAL
CIDER
ABV 6.0%
BEAUTIFULLY SIMPLE

BLACKCURRANT

-DECIDERLY GOOD-
APPLE COUNTY
CIDER CO
CIDER WITH A DASH OF BLACKCURRANT
BLACKCURRANT
4.0% vol.
330ml

APPLE COUNTY CIDER CO
BLACKCURRANT

Nestling on the Welsh/English borders is Apple County Cider Co, founded by husband and wife team Ben and Steph Culpin, amid the rich soils and mellow climate between Skenfrith and Monmouth.

Known for crafting single varietals with style – you don't get Great Taste's top Golden Fork award twice in a row on a whim – Ben attributes this to his honed sense of taste. 'My palate is my number one friend,' he says as we sip through the range. It's an early spring day and Ben and Steph's dogs, Pippin and Wurzel, are soaking up the faint sunlight.

We're discussing favourite apples. 'Dabinett is unique,' says Ben, explaining how he loves its full body and hint of spice. His Dabinett's abv is north of 6%, suggesting dilution isn't top of the agenda.

Vilberie is another favourite, and it was this that won their first Golden Fork awards. 'It holds its own,' says Steph. 'Bold aromas yet light and refreshing to taste.'

Ben began his cidermaking career in earnest with brother Alex and stepfather, the late Jimmy McConnell, with Ty Gwyn back in the late 2000s. Ty Gwyn now rests with Alex in the next door valley with its own welcoming Cider Shop and Bar. Ben and Steph, meanwhile, are focusing on Monmouthshire's place as 'the apple county of Wales'.

Apple County Cider Co's fruit ciders arrived relatively recently. They have an exceptional balance, an ability to combine cider's tang with the natural, tart flavours of the fruit without masking either with unwarranted sweetness. The blackcurrants offer amazing richness plus a little boost on the tannin front.

England's blackcurrant heartland of Pixley, just over the border in Herefordshire, is responsible for the Culpins' blackcurrants. Sometimes borders have benefits.

region: Monmouthshire, Wales

fruit: Michelin, the reliable bittersweet variety; unsweetened blackcurrant juice, fresh pressed and cold stored

life story: October/ November harvest, slow fermentation in the barn for up to seven months; blackcurrant juice added at end of fermentation; sugar addition kept deliberately small

abv: 4%

if you like this: try Rhubarb, Dabinett, Vilberie, Perry

experience: visit shop, summer opening, check the website; Orchard Walk; pre-book tutored Tastings & Tours or Picnic Vouchers; Abergavenny Food Festival, September; Welsh Cider & Perry Festival, May

applecountycider.co.uk

KILMEGAN
REAL CIDER

region: County Down, Northern Ireland

fruit: a blend of bittersweet and dessert varieties from County Down, Armagh and Tipperary

life story: with a variety of harvest dates, Dabinett and Michelin are pressed together, the later season varieties similarly blended and pressed; fermented through to dryness; blended in tank seven months before bottling, with small apple juice addition to sweeten

abv: 6.8%

if you like this: try Irish Farmhouse; Elderflower

experience: Belfast Beer & Cider Festival, November; check website for pubs, bars and shops stocking Kilmegan

kilmegancider.com

Over 50 years ago, Andrew Boyd's father Maurice stumbled upon an ancient orchard planted generations before, near his family's new home, a farmstead just outside the historic seaside town of Dundrum in Northern Ireland. Inspired by memories of Maurice making apple wine, in 2009 Andrew and his wife Karen resurrected his little old wine press and had a go themselves.

Their new cider proved to be a lightbulb moment. Here was something elegant with fine tannins, a world away from commercial offerings. Just seven years later Andrew beat off hundreds of other contenders to walk off with the 2016 Reserve Supreme Champion at the Royal Bath & West Show.

In the meantime he'd honed his process, worked on his apple blends and upgraded his equipment. As you'd imagine for someone with a horticulture background, he's using a complex mix of varieties. While Armagh is known for Bramleys in particular, other varieties do thrive, but it's to Tipperary that Andrew heads for much of his bittersweet fruit.

The Kilmegan blends include classics such as Dabinett and Michelin, newer dessert apples like Katy, Jonagold and Jona Prince, plus less well-known varieties such as Falstaff. Even the French bittersweet, Bedan – 'it adds this buttery vanilla note on the aroma' – makes an appearance.

Real Cider is elegant, dry and eloquent, with very fine tannins and flavours, including a hint of peach and Russet. We are tasting in Andrew's cosy tasting room, matching with local cheeses. Then Andrew mentions Sean Doyle's cider, apple and leek cream sauce recipe for pressed pork belly at the Maghera Inn, near Newcastle, and it's hard to turn back. Perhaps not unexpectedly, Kilmegan cider has found its way into many of Northern Ireland's top restaurants. Provenance leads the way.

KILMEGAN
IRISH CIDER
Real
CIDER
DRY
"for the purist"
500ml℮
Contains Natural Sediments
ABV 6.8%

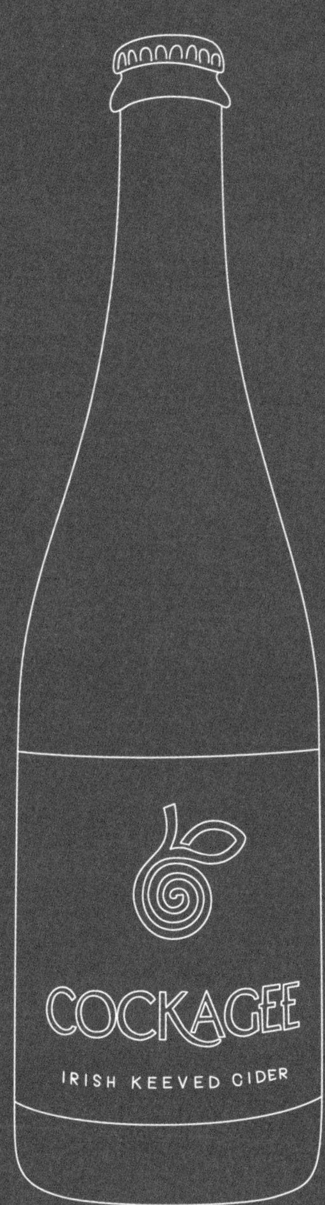
COCKAGEE
IRISH KEEVED CIDER

THE CIDER MILL
COCKAGEE

Mark Jenkinson is on a mission. To rediscover the historic Irish apple variety, Cockagee. Queen Victoria apparently paid four times the going rate for this apple. And he might well have done so, tracking down its alter ego in England, the beautifully named Hens' Turds (well, Cockagee is Irish for goose turds, referring to the yellow-green colour of the apple, just so we're on the same page).

Along the way, Mark has nurtured an orchard with over 120 varieties of apple. In there are classics from France and England as well as Ireland. And he's the only one in Ireland to use the keeving method for his cider, perhaps not surprisingly called, you guessed it, Cockagee.

Dark amber in the glass, there's a real complexity and fine balance. The variety of apple flavours is enchanting, the acids are subtle, but just enough to balance, and the tannins are subtly evident, transported by a gentle natural sparkle. Toffee notes combine with baked apple, raisins and demerara on the palate, with the sparkle giving a crisp finish.

Mark is a stained glass artist with several decades of experience. 'I first started by making apple juice for my kids,' he says. 'The natural next step was cider. I have always played around with fermentations – beer, kombucha, cheesemaking. I'm fascinated by yeasts, moulds and bacteria, and how almost all our food and drink rely on this micro-wildlife!'

Keeving came under scrutiny for the same reason: 'A fascination with a highly unusual and mysterious natural process reliant on our micro friends, and the challenge of trying to learn how the process works.' He's a driven man.

region: Boyne Valley, Ireland

fruit: a blend from Mark's orchards and others nearby; 65–85% cider varieties, 15–35% 'older, flavoursome dessert varieties'

life story: produced using the keeving method to retain natural sweetness, with a six to eight month fermentation, hand bottled and matured in the bottle for six months

abv: 5%

if you like this: try Cockagee Perry, the new Revival Series: Ciderkin, Windvane, Lamhog

experience: contact ahead for group tours and tasting at the farm; watch the website for summer food and drink events

thecidermill.ie

LLEWELLYNS
VINTAGE CIDER 2014, FRIZZANTE

region: County Dublin, Ireland

fruit: Pinova

life story: cool, slow fermentation and malolactic fermentation with wild yeast; secondary bottle fermentation, ageing on lees for one year

abv: 8.3%

if you like this: try Double L Bone Dry Cider, unsweetened bittersweet/dessert blend

experience: find David at farmers' markets: Temple Bar Food Market, Dublin; People's Park, Dún Laoghaire; see website for cidermaking courses, juice sold for cidermaking; Sheridans Irish Food Festival, County Meath, May

llewellynsorchard.ie

If we hadn't already been expecting something a little different from David Llewellyn, the frosted bottle with hand-drawn label certainly got us prepared.

A boutique cider producer, he is also Ireland's only commercial winemaker, with a nice line in cider vinegar too. And the cider doesn't disappoint. Palest yellow in colour, the fragrance and floral notes lead the way. With tangerine, lemon and lime zest, it's incredibly wine-like. There's a lively texture and light orangey zest notes on the close.

It's made using the apple Pinova, aka Piñata. This is a relatively young variety originally from Germany with class in its parentage, including Golden Delicious, Cox's Orange Pippin, and the historic Duchess of Oldenburg.

'I liked that the apple was very sweet and had amazing flavours,' said David, explaining why he chose to make a single varietal. 'I just felt from eating the fruit that this could make an interesting cider, even if it were to be a one-off.'

Coincidentally, it was Germany that sparked David's interest in all things fermentation. He was on a work placement, having finished his horticulture degree. 'By accident I found myself immersed in the field of viticulture and oenology which resulted in me getting bitten by the winemaking bug,' he explains.

Back in Ireland, David set up his fruit-growing business at the turn of the century just on the outskirts of Dublin. Slowly but surely, this has grown in scope, and you'll find a variety of produce at the two farmers' markets he frequents.

His is a straightforward philosophy: 'A quality, pure-juice cider is as worthy of the same status and respect that is conferred on a decent wine.' In his hands, it certainly is.

Llewellyns
Vintage
Cider
2014
Frizzante
750 ml
8.3 %
David Llewellyn, Quickpenny Road, Lusk,
Co. Dublin, Ireland. Tel: +353-87-2843879
www.llewellynsorchard.ie

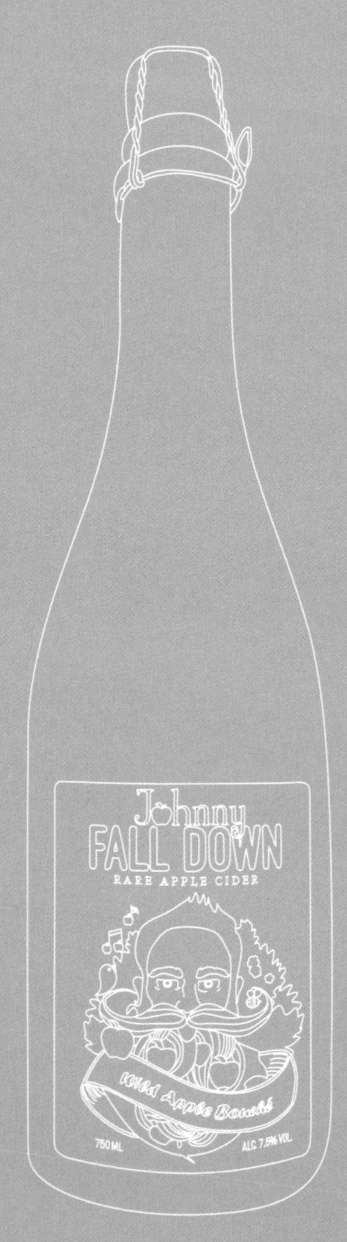
Johnny
FALL DOWN
RARE APPLE CIDER
Wild Apple Bouché
750 ML
ALC 7.5% VOL

JOHNNY FALL DOWN
WILD APPLE BOUCHÉ, 2016

'We grafted the bejesus out of it!' Barry Walsh, co-founder of Killahora Orchards, is talking about one of the wild trees that provided fruit for Johnny Fall Down Wild Apple Bouché, the 2018 Bath & West International Cider Champion.

Killahora Orchards currently has over 100 different varieties of apple, 'I know, it's too many!' admits Barry, trying to shift the blame to co-founder, cousin David. 'He is the tree geek.'

While Killahora Orchards only began selling in the last few years, some of the trees they harvest from are over 100 years old. Indeed, this area near Cork has strong apple history; an 1837 Ordnance Survey map of the estate depicts orchards, and an 1833 tithe book mentions a taxed orchard.

To add to this, with David's father Tim guiding matters, they planted an orchard seven years ago, deliberately choosing rare and unusual varieties as well as standards.

And it turns out, the hedgerows are fruitful too. David was convinced there was something interesting in one such hedgerow. Sure enough, when they finished beating off the nettles they discovered a dozen wild apple trees. They fermented the apples from each separately to see what the potential might be.

Three were pure acids. 'Good for correcting other ferments,' says Barry. Five were pretty good, but four were outstanding. And it's these which make up nearly half of Wild Apple Bouché, 2016.

Beautiful and crafted, this has great depth, boasting cooked and fresh fruit notes, with perceptible tannins pleasingly present. Just off-dry, the sparkle is well judged. While this is from a very small batch, it will appear again. And providing the grafts take, in a few years' time the batches might not be so small.

Killahora Orchards

region: County Cork, Ireland

fruit: just under half are wild, unnamed trees, a small amount of ice cider, made from non-tannin apples, added to help raise the alcohol level, plus a mix of cider and dessert varieties

life story: harvested and pressed as usual; cool fermentation; blending before bottling with some residual sugar for the secondary fermentation

abv: 7.5%

if you like this: try Johnny Fall Down Bittersweet; Rare Apple Ice Wine

experience: check Twitter and Instagram for news of events

killahoraorchards.ie

LONGUEVILLE HOUSE CIDER

region: County Cork, Ireland

fruit: Dabinett, Michelin cider apples

life story: natural yeast, four-month fermentation, ten months ageing prior to bottling, backsweetening with Bramley/ Norfolk Royal Russet/Katy juice

abv: 5.5%

if you like this: try Mór; Irish Apple Brandy

experience: visit House for Blossom to Bottle, Walk, Talk & Taste, May; harvest lunch, October; group tours available

longuevillehouse.ie

Before the Magners phenomenon was a twinkle in a marketeer's eye, Longueville House near Cork was planting apple trees. Not just dessert-apple trees, cider varieties.

Longueville House sits in the picturesque Blackwater Valley, just south of Cork. Returned into the hands of its founding family, the O'Callaghans, in the 1930s after several centuries with the Longfords/ Longuevilles, it was Michael O'Callaghan who took the orchard plunge in 1985.

Admittedly, it was more to follow his love of brandy and Calvados than a passion for cider. Thus vines were also planted, but it was the trees that did well. Michael proved to be quite the pioneer, becoming the first person in over 100 years to distil cider – legally, that is!

Proudly declaring 'from blossom to bottle', Michael's son William is in charge now with this wife Aisling, with Dan Duggan in the master distiller and chief ciderologist role.

And what of the cider? Pouring cloudy in the glass, there's an explosion of rich, sweet tannins on the medium-dry palate, alongside rich caramel notes. Flavours of cooked apples and apricots sit alongside the typical palate-drying astringency of Dabinett and Michelin, a popular duo when it comes to planting and crafting true ciders. Natural yeast and a four month fermentation add to the breadth and depth of flavours.

There's a bigger brother to this cider, helpfully called Mór, where the original cider spends six months in Longueville Apple Brandy casks before bottling.

'We are aiming to produce an uninterfered-with, tasty cider which speaks of the *terroir* it comes from, the Blackwater Valley,' William tells me. I'd say that's job done, then.

LH
Longueville
House
Cider

FRANCE

France wears its cider production proudly along its western and northern shores, with pockets further south towards the Loire Valley. The Celtic-infused coastline boasts a rich tapestry of cider as well as dessert-apple varieties, with the earliest written references dating back to the 11th century. By the late 1500s, research was already ongoing into cider apples in Normandy.

While over 1,000 apple cultivars are recognised, each region has its own favoured varieties, as well as a number – including the bittersweet Douce Moën and the bitter Marie Ménard – that perform well wherever.

In the early 20th century, as wars took their toll, the cider and apple-growing communities faced hardships. Central government called for orchards to be uprooted in the 1950s, but the regions fought back.

Take Brittany. A community of orchardists and cidermakers in Finistère on the west coast formed CIDREF in the 1980s, the idea being to safeguard and champion both trees and the ciders they produced. Campaigning secured its own protected designation of origin (PDO), Cornouaille, in 1996. Fiercely proud of its Breton and its Celtic heritage – watch out for the bands of bagpipers during the Cornouaille Festival – apple varieties have magical-sounding names and distinct identities. Allowing around 30 varieties in a typical blend, Cornouaille also stipulates allowed yields from the various orchard types.

The other French cider PDO is Pays d'Auge in Normandy. Here in the land of Calvados and Camembert, tall trees on traditional rootstocks share space with herds of grazing cows. Thanks to the Calvados involvement, there are striking destinations to visit. None more so than Christian Drouin, with

EXPLORE

CIDREF: cidref.fr

IDAC: idac-aoc.fr/index.php/en/les-cidres-aop.html

National Institute of Origin and Quality: inao.gouv.fr

Poiré Domfront PDO: poire-domfront.fr

Musée du Poiré, Barenton: parc-naturel-normandie-maine.fr/decouvrir/musee_du_poire.html

Cider Route, Pays d'Auge: calvados-tourisme.co.uk/en/discover/tourist-trails/the-cider-route.php

La Fête des Pommiers Fouesnant, July

Cornouaille Festival, July: festival-cornouaille.bzh/en

La Route du Poiré, Orne, Normandy

Fête du Poiré, Domfront, July

Fête du Cidre, Pays d'Auge, October

La Fête de la Pomme, October: ville-fouesanant.fr/fete-de-la-pomme-2017

Mark Gleonec, president Cornouaille PDO, macgleo.com

beautiful orchards surrounding historic buildings, each tree not only named but explained.

Fifty of the 750 known Norman varieties can be used in the PDO cider, and around two-thirds of the blend must be bitter/bittersweet varieties.

What characterises much of French cider is keeving, the tricky process by which ciders retain some sweetness without the addition of sugar or further juice (see page 221).

These regions boast many personalities. Eric Bordelet, the former Michelin-starred sommelier, broke free of regulations to craft exquisitely fine-boned *sidres* and *poirés*. More recently, Cyril Zangs is picking up the freestyle mantle with his uncompromising approach to quality and his serried ranks of bottle-fermenting ciders. Meanwhile, newcomer Nicolas Poirier is making his mark in Morbihan with Distillerie du Gorvello.

And what about perry? Domfront in Normandy is a valiant stronghold, with the Poiré Domfront PDO/AOP laying claim to around 100,000 pear trees in over 100 different varieties. Producers like Pacory and Ferme de l'Yonnière work hard to nurture and sustain these gracious giants.

The French challenge is to move perceptions beyond the *crêperie* and onto the dining table. Places like Le Sistrot in Quimper, western Brittany, with brothers Ronan and Erwan Gire, show the way. As my charming Breton host, the pony-tailed Cornouaille president Mark Gleonec, says, *A wir galon*. Cheers!

ERIC BORDELET
SYDRE ARGELETTE, 2015

region: Mayenne, Normandy

fruit: over 20 varieties. 'It's like being a parent; you can't choose a favourite apple'

life story: selective harvest as and when ripe; apples kept for three to five weeks before gentle pressing; *méthode ancestrale*, slow fermentation; bottled with some residual sugar to develop sparkle in the bottle

abv: 5.5%

if you like this: try Poiré Granit, made with 15 varieties of perry pears from old trees; Sydre Brut

experience: contact Eric's stockists at home and abroad – three-quarters is exported to over 20 countries

ericbordelet.com/ english

ericbordelet.com

'You have to be at one with the ecosystem, your varieties, your ground. You're the conductor of the orchestra. You have to compose the music.'

Eric Bordelet, former Michelin-starred Parisian sommelier and the original French cider *terroiriste*, is explaining how his friend, the late Didier Dagueneau, influenced his cidermaking philosophy. 'He opened many boxes for me,' says Eric about Dagueneau, an instinctive Loire winemaker famous for championing biodynamism and focusing on the soils. 'I learnt a lot with him. Don't trust too much what others say. Just decide yourself. Do many trials.'

And that's the way Eric has been making his name since he returned to the family farm in the southern Normandy borders in the early 1990s. Rather than stay with tradition he took the then radical step of treating cider like wine, apples like grapes. Instead of obeying rules and following formulae – 'I don't like control' – he chose apples he felt would work well in blends. He nurtured his orchard, consulting François Bouchet, the godfather of biodynamic viticulture in France, early on.

And he looked to the ground, naming his flagship cider – or *sydre*, as he calls it – Argelette, using the old spelling, after one of the soil types beneath his feet on the Normandy/Loire border.

Today he cherishes over 20 varieties of apple, planting more each year, always standard-size trees. Pears too get the forensic treatment.

Sydre Argelette is crafted from all the apple varieties he grows. With peach and ripe apricots on the nose, it follows through to more stone fruit flavours alongside rustic Russet and Braeburn apple-type notes across the palate. The texture is elegant, with gently present tannins and a long finish. It's like a cider symphony.

SYDRE
ARGELETTE
Eric Bordelet

CONCOURS GÉNÉRAL AGRICOLE
MÉDAILLE DE BRONZE
PARIS 2017
MINISTÈRE DE L'AGRICULTURE ET DE L'ALIMENTATION
PRODUIT DE FRANCE
CIDRERIE DE MENEZ-BRUG
Cornouaille
APPELLATION CORNOUAILLE PROTÉGÉE
Cidre des Vergers de Fouesnant
MIS EN BOUTEILLE À LA PROPRIÉTÉ
STEVEN GOENVEC • 54 HENT CARBON
F-29170 FOUESNANT • FRANCE
Graet e Breizh
Steven Goenvec

CIDRERIE DE MENEZ-BRUG
CORNOUAILLE, 2016

It was a busy morning the day we visited Menez-Brug, within minutes of the beautiful Fouesnant coastline in mid-western Brittany. I am with my gracious Breton guide, Mark Gleonec, president of CIDREF, the Cornouaille 'cidricultural' association. With its warm wood panelling, friendly tables and handy bar from which to sample the Goenvec family's ciders, the tasting room was bustling.

Claude Goenvec set up Menez-Brug in the late 1980s, nurturing it until he handed it over to his children Steven and Lénaïg in 2013. Even before he went commercial though, Claude had made his mark in the Breton cider world. Claude had been among the founding members of CIDREF, with its quest to safeguard the culture of cidermaking in Cornouaille. In 1996, the association secured PDO status for Cornouaille, the only Breton region to do so.

'It's always interesting, the changing of the seasons,' Steven says, when I ask what he enjoys the most. With cider training at Le Robillard in Normandy on top of winemaking college, he brings a broad perspective.

Wandering with him through the orchards, it's clear Steven has inherited his father's passion for apples. His descriptions of the local varieties, including the pride of Fouesnant, C'hwerv-brizh (pronounced *fero-brij*), conjure up vivid images of their qualities.

This is reflected in the glass. Golden bronze in colour and off-dry with a fine sparkle, the palate is elegant and rich, with apricot and peach mousse notes. There's a good balance between a gentle astringency and a soft sweetness, reminiscent of Cox apples on a warm summer's evening, plus a honeyed hint and a lightly caramelised note on the finish. 'Ample and fruity', was how Mark described it when we headed to the bar. Too true.

Appellation Cornouaille Protégée

region: Cornouaille, Brittany

fruit: a blend of four local apples, including C'hwerv-brizh and the sweet Douce-bloc'hig (pronounced *douce blorig*)

life story: apples are blended before crushing; natural yeast, unless cultured also required; the fermenting juice is keeved; cool six-month fermentation; natural sparkle retained in the bottle via transfer method

abv: 4.5%

if you like this: try Cidre de Fouesnant

experience: visit the shop, confirm times by phone; La Fête des Pommiers, Fouesnant, July; follow the Route du Cidre Cornouaille

bretoncellar.com/cidery-menez-brug

KERMAO
CIDRE CORNOUAILLE, 2017

Appellation Cornouaille Protégée

region: Cornouaille, Britanny

fruit: a blend of five apples approved by Cornouaille PDO, plus a little Guillevic

life story: harvested apples are pre-mixed before pressing; the juice undergoes keeving before fermentation, finishing in the bottle; yeast removed via the transfer method

abv: 4.5%

if you like this: try La Fouesnant, demi-sec; Le Kermao, brut

experience: enjoy a taste and a chat at La Cidrerie, Monday–Saturday, check website for times; orchard visit, Friday, May–September; pre-booking required October–April and for groups

www.cidre-bretagne.com

Kermao's Cidre Cornouaille 2017 speaks volumes not only about the region's apples and their complexity but also the approach taken at harvest. Owners Brieug and Marine Saliou sell off apples picked at the start of harvest so they can focus their attention on the ones with the right flavour credentials.

Based roughly in the centre of the Cornouaille region but still less than half-an-hour from the coast, harvest itself is both by hand and machine. Some varieties then wait 2–3 weeks before pressing.

The Salious grow over a dozen varieties, all Cornouaille specialities, including a few favourites such as bittersweets Kroc'henn-ki, Douce Moën, and Prat-yeot, the bittersharp Kermerrien plus a few tannic varieties, Marie Ménard and Douce-koed-ligne.

Their Cidre Cornouaille is a beautiful clear gold colour, with a minute bead of bubbles tracing its way up the glass. Aromas of exceptionally ripe, fresh apples mix with cooked apple and exotic honey notes on the nose. There's a well-poised balance between sweetness and gentle, apple snow-like tannins. Ripe and tart peaches add up to a lingering, clean finish, which is again honeyed without being cloying.

Brieug's parents Yves and Jacqueline established Kermao in 1991 having made cider before as a hobby. 'My parents had the farm but were working in a bank,' Steven explains. Proud members of the Cornouaille 'cidricultural' alliance CIDREF, Kermao actively supports the ongoing trials with potential new blends from old varieties from the CIDREF experimental orchard. 'We don't want them to disappear,' says Marine. She and Brieug have also added a further 7ha (17 acres) of orchards since taking over.

'We're planting for tomorrow,' she continues. The future suddenly seems a whole lot brighter.

PRODUIT DE FRANCE
KERMAO
CIDRE
CORNOUAILLE
Appellation Cornouaille Protégée
4,5%vol.
2017
75cl
Mis en bouteille à la propriété
Les Vergers de Kermao
29950 Gouesnac'h
Propriétaire - Récoltant
www.cidre-bretagne.com
Lot1 - Contient des sulfites - Effervescence naturelle
Médaille d'Argent
Concours Régional 2017
International Cider & Perry Competition
2017

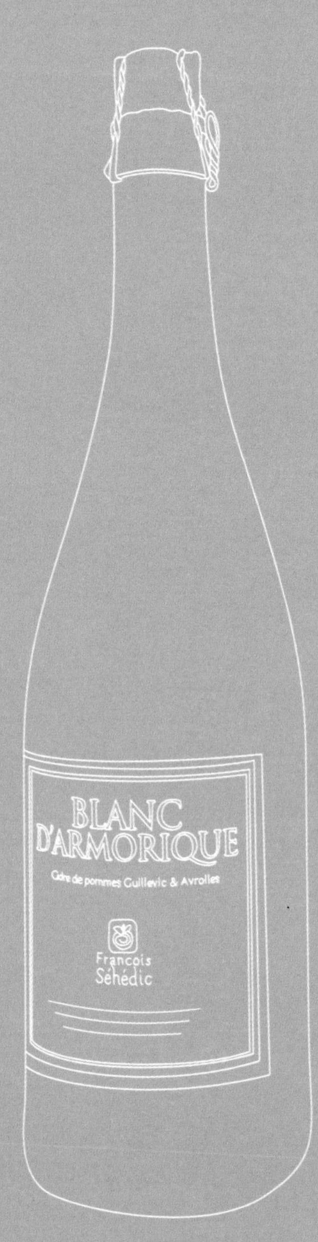
BLANC
D'ARMORIQUE
Cidre de pommes Guillevic & Avrolles
François
Séhédic

SÉHÉDIC
BLANC D'ARMORIQUE, 2016

We're at the oldest cidery in the Fouesnant region. Founded by François Séhédic in 1950, Christian Daniélou currently holds the reins along with his wife, Marie Laure Séhédic. A former accountant of 25-years' standing, Christian has acclimatised well to his new profession.

'It is better to make cider with a large number of apples,' says Christian. He and Marie Laure grow 35 varieties in their 18ha (45 acres) of orchards. Spread over three sites, the orchards are all organic.

There's an array of ciders on offer at the homely – and handy – tasting room/farm shop in the centre of Forêt-Fouesnant. The selection includes Séhédic Brut, the most popular, and its Extra Brut, a first for the region, plus an award-winning range of lambig (cider brandy) and pommeau.

My guide, Mark Gleonec and I, have been inspired, however, by the Blanc d'Armorique, a blend of the forever fragrant, sometimes exotic Guillevic and the less well known, equally aromatic and more tangy Avrolles. Responsible for the sparkling ciders often kept for Sundays, Guillevic was sometimes called the 'champagne of Brittany'. Once on the endangered list, it took the efforts of orchardists and cidermakers, particularly in Morbihan further south towards the borders with the Loire (see Cidrerie Nicol, page 73) to revive the fortunes of this beguiling apple.

Christian crafted this pairing with seafood in mind. After all, we are but minutes away from the abundance of the Atlantic coast.

Very pale in colour, this is complex but refined and exquisitely fragrant too, with hints of candy and candied orange; apricots, peaches and tangerine glide over the palate. Sparkling, pure and clear, citrus zest finishes the experience. A modern twist on a traditional craft.

region: Cornouaille, Brittany

fruit: a blend of Guillevic and Avrolles, both sweet, sharp cider varieties

life story: harvest in early autumn, milling and pressing; keeving and cool temperature fermentation; secondary fermentation via the *charmat* method

abv: 5.5%

if you like this: try Extra Brut; Gwennic; Traditionnel

experience: visit shop/tasting room, check website for days/opening hours; Séhédic is available in USA, Germany, Italy

cidre-sehedic.fr

MANOIR DU KINKIZ
CORNOUAILLE, 2016

Appellation Cornouaille Contrôlée

region: Cornouaille, Brittany

fruit: a blend created from the Cornouaille-PDO approved range of apples

life story: the juice is keeved before three-to-four-month fermentation in tank, bottling with some residual sugar and yeast to finish fermentation in the bottle

abv: 5%

if you like this: try the zesty Manoir du Kinkiz Cuvée Blanche, crafted from Guillevic, with its grapefruit and exotic stone fruits

experience: visit the cellars, see the vintage harvesting displays, taste the selection, including a well-regarded pommeau and lambig range

cidre-kinkiz.fr

'That's Marie Ménard. A very strong red [colour]. Some are white, like Douce Moën.' This is Hervé Seznec. We are gazing up at a stained glass window, with its striking image of apple blossom, in the atmospheric cellar at Manoir de Kinkiz, the cidery and distillery run by Hervé and his wife Morgane. We're near Quimper in Cornouaille, Britanny's sole AOP region, in Finistère, and we've just returned after wandering through Hervé's trial orchard, with its 25 varieties of cider-apple tree.

While the Manoir is on the site of an ancient castle, the cider story began here in the 1970s. The farm used to be a dairy but as the apple took over, Hervé's father Pierre became wedded to the cause. Not wanting to see any more local apple varieties disappear in the wake of the French government's plans to reshape farms, he became the founding president of CIDREF, the 'cidricultural' alliance which champions cidermaking in Finistère.

They say, 'Like father, like son', and Hervé is visibly animated as he describes the apples in his various blends.

The Cornouaille 2016 we are tasting, for example, has the Marie Ménard depicted in the window, plus other local heroes, including the bittersweet Kermerrien and sweet Douce Moën.

And it has lovely breadth and depth, with peach, apricot and tangerine flavours. Golden in colour, the tannins are rich and fulsome. There's a fine bubble beading through, and it's this plus the depth of the fruit that drives a lengthy finish.

Fiercely organic, Hervé blends the apples before pressing. 'When you extract the tannins and the flavour, the blends of the varieties give more fruit flavour,' he explains. The Marie Ménard will be making its presence felt again, I'd wager.

APPELLATION CORNOUAILLE CONTROLEE

PUR JUS

PROPRIÉTAIRE
RÉCOLTANT

HERVÉ SEZNEC
Ergué-Armel
29000 QUIMPER
Tél : 02 98 90 20 57

Manoir du Kinkiz

L.01

75 cl

dans ce cidre
à effervescence naturelle
un léger dépôt est possible
Produit de France

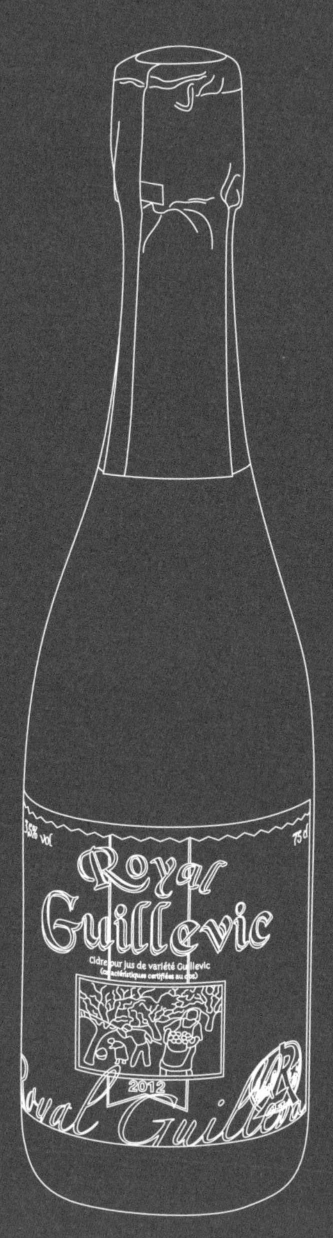
3,5% vol
75 cl
Royal Guillevic
Cidre pur jus de variété Guillevic
2012

CIDRERIE NICOL
ROYAL GUILLEVIC, LABEL ROUGE

The feeling of pride is palpable as we walk through Jean-Michel Nicol's orchard. For 90 years his family has been making cider from Breton apple varieties. Jean-Michel and his brother Didier are the third generation to pick up the baton.

Based in Morbihan in southern Brittany ('small sea' in Breton, named after the local landmark), the region is best known on the tourist trail for its ancient stones which predate Stonehenge.

Jean-Michel's great-uncle André set up the *cidrerie*, but it wasn't until the 1980s that André's nephew Jean took the decision to focus on cider, when the European milk lake gave the cows a reprieve. Today Cidrerie Nicol – also known as Cidres de Rhuys, after the peninsular where it is located – produces a selection of ciders, ranging from off-dry to sweet, with the sparkling Royal Guillevic and its *Label Rouge* badge of honour arguably the star of the team.

The climate in Morbihan is milder than that of its northern neighbours, providing the *cidrerie*'s secret ingredient: more sun to ripen the Guillevic apple, a small, green variety known for its fragrance, tang and charm.

With lemon, tangerine, apricot, peach and floral notes on the nose, Royal Guillevic is sprightly and elegant. The palate is complex, with flavours of yellow melon, pears and yellow apple notes, plus a lengthy finish.

There are 15 beehives to help with pollination, the family has operated a bottle return and re-use system for a decade and, after pressing, the pulp goes off to either compost or biogas production. Environmental awareness has always been important to Jean-Michel. No wonder he is smiling.

region: Morbihan, Brittany

fruit: the sharp Guillevic cider variety

life story: following a three-month initial fermentation, the second fermentation takes place in tank before bottling

abv: 3.5%

if you like this: look for Cidre de Rhuys Doux, with its Breton blend, including popular Douce Moën, Bedon and Kroc'hen ki varieties

experience: head to the crêperies of Brittany for this and other Cidrerie Nicol ciders; you'll also find it in London, North America, the Far East and in Europe

cidres-nicol.bzh

DISTILLERIE DU GORVELLO
COCO D'ISSÉ

Cidre Artisanal de Bretagne

region: Morbihan, Brittany

fruit: the bittersharp variety, Coco d'Issé, rescued from extinction, one of the all-Breton cast in Nicolas' orchards

life story: Nicolas waits for the apples to fall, believing it's better for quality and aromatics; selected yeast for secondary bottle fermentation; undisgorged

abv: 3%

if you like this: try dry Heritage blend, including Marie Ménard, one of Nicolas' favourite varieties, crafted to go with seafood

experience: visit the cidery, children join the tastings with three different apple juices; tours July–Aug; all year for groups

distilleriedu gorvello.fr

Phoenix-like, Coco d'Issé has returned from near extinction to the orchards of Morbihan in southern Brittany.

Nicolas Poirier, the genial yet driven ciderista behind Distillerie du Gorvello's recent re-emergence as a vital force in Breton cidermaking, took scions from five trees and now there are 800 planted up.

But why? For this extraordinary pinky golden cider in my glass. With a nose of candied pineapple, papaya and mango, the palate is all fuzzy peach, more candied fruit, with a persistent but gentle sparkle, good acidity and a honeyed after-taste. The acids are there to balance, but there is also honeysuckle, rosemary honey and papaya. Some cherry and raspberry flavours too.

Alongside a modern cidery with stainless steel tanks, 25 Shropshire sheep have joined the team. Firmly organic but not biodynamic, Nicolas uses sprays with oligo elements and essential oils to ward off diseases. Being in the driest part of Brittany helps, but Nicolas is aware of global warming. Since he arrived in 2012, the date of harvest has moved a month earlier.

Coming from a family with winemaking on one side and a restaurant on the other, Nicolas wanted to craft something himself. 'Since I was very young, I was very interested in gastronomic things,' he says. 'I'm not from Brittany, but it's my favourite region in France. The strong identity. The landscape. The sea.'

Recently elected as president of the regional cidermakers' alliance, The Cider House of Brittany, Nicolas feels honoured. Determined, with charm, he has one last request.

'Please put in your book: 100% juice.' With pleasure.

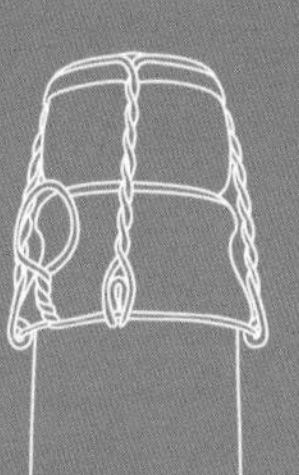

Distillerie du Gorvello
CIDRE ARTISANAL
DE BRETAGNE
INDICATION GÉOGRAPHIQUE PROTÉGÉE
Coco d'Issé
PRESSÉ, ÉLEVÉ ET MIS EN BOUTEILLE À LA PROPRIÉTÉ
PAR NICOLAS POIRIER, PRODUCTEUR-TRANSFORMATEUR
75 CL - 3% VOL

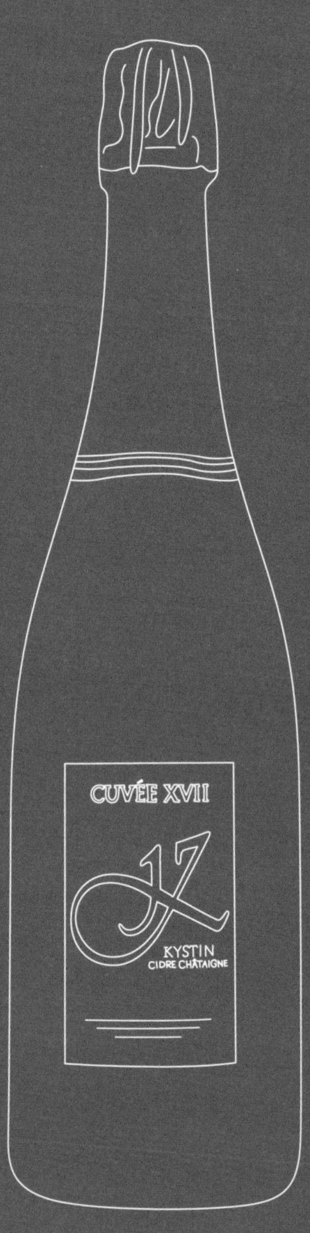
CUVÉE XVII
17
KYSTIN
CIDRE CHÂTAIGNE

KYSTIN
CUVÉE XVII 2016, CIDRE CHÂTAIGNE

With over a decade in the cider industry in both Normandy and Brittany, it could have gone either way for Sasha Crommar when he decided to strike out on his own. A safe, reliable cider, like all the others. Or something that little bit different. Chat to Sasha for five minutes, with his focused gaze and detailed yet creative delivery, and you'll know which way he went. Yep – the 'road less travelled' for him.

'I like to cook. I have lots of my friends with Michelin stars, and they said, "your ciders are good – make something different." I remembered, I really like apple compote, and when I put chestnut purée inside, I thought "Yes, the taste is good."'

So how to make that work in cidermaking? It took a while to suss it out. Eventually, Sasha realised he had to ferment the cider together with the crushed chestnuts after the *chapeau brun* stage of keeving.

Thus Cuvée XVII was his first cider. Watery gold in colour with a light to medium sparkle, there are beautiful aromas of praline and marzipan, thanks in part to the low temperature at which fermentation takes place, around 6°C (43°F). Fine, dusky tannins tease the palate, which offers up notes of crushed fresh walnuts on top of ripe, autumnal apples.

I first tried this at Le Sistrot, Ronan Gire's peerless restaurant with a 50-plus cider list in Quimper, Britanny. While Ronan pairs XVII with his autumnal menus in particular, my feeling is that with its sparkly, unique flavour profile, it's a cider for all seasons.

Sasha should be proud.

region: Brittany/ Normandy

fruit: special blend of 16 bitter, sweet, sharp and bittersweet apples; the chestnut is the XVII ingredient

life story: apples harvested in December; milled and pressed, crushed chestnuts added into freshly keeved juice, fermented for 10 months, 3–6°C (37–43°F)

abv: 4%

if you like this: try Kalysïe, Kystin's ginger poiré, named in honour of *Game of Thrones'* Khaleesi; Classic Opalyne, crafted with crêpes in mind

experience: visit Kystin shop in Vannes; visit Crêperie Keroyal, Plougomelen, Vannes; save up for Alexandre Couillon's 2-Michelin star Restaurant La Marine, Noirmoutier, off the Breton coast

kystin.net

PACORY
POIRÉ DOMFRONT L'IDÉAL, 2015

Appellation d'Origine Protegée

region: Domfrontais, Normandy

fruit: organic Plant de Blancs perry pears from trees over 100 years old, low-density planting of 30 trees per ha (12 per acre)

life story: depending on how ripe the pears are at harvest defines how long they spend macerating before pressing; fresh juice is cooled for several days to develop further aromas; pressing is slow; natural fermentation, with second fermentation in bottle

abv: 4.5%

if you like this: try Poiré Domfront Classic; Poiré Fermier

experience: take the Poiré Route; Pacory can be found in Germany, Sweden, Finland and Denmark, plus Japan, USA and New Zealand

pacory.eu

'The best teacher was my father.' Simon Pacory is explaining how, with no specific school for poiré in France, he learnt the art of making *poiré* at winemaking school in nearby Angers and at home with dad.

We are in the heart of Domfrontais, the epicentre of French *poiré* culture. With its deep clay and granite sub-soils it's somewhere for pear trees rather than apples to excel.

In Normandy, perhaps as we are slap bang in cheese country, it's cows that graze the fields and not sheep, so tall trees are the norm. Calvados is important at Pacory, but not to the detriment of *poiré*.

Yet trees the size of houses are never going to be fast money-spinners – Simon recounts the saying about perry pear trees: 100 years to grow, 100 to produce, 100 to die. So even Domfrontais has had to trigger its own rescue mission in recent decades to redeem the culture of perry from oblivion.

We are at Ferme des Grimaux with one of the region's leading families. Simon's parents, Frédéric and Catherine, inherited trees and have also been responsible for increasing their plantings considerably. It's a beautiful, organic setting. The drama and grace of the majestic perry trees even in their naked, wintry stage, is bewitching. The Pacorys' dog Gypsy leads the way.

With three levels of quality, we have the highest, L'idéal, here. Honeyed scents mix with ripe pears while the palate is light, off-dry and with its own fine pear character. Ripe Comice-type flavours appear alongside *tarte aux poires* notes, a light starfruit tang offering a green counterpoint. Pear-skin notes add to the length and breadth. I think those were lessons well taught.

Poiré
Domfront
2015
Poiré
Domfront
Appellation d'Origine Protégée
L'idéal
Ferme des Grimaux
PACORY
61350 MANTILLY

Poiré Fermier
Issu de Vergers Traditionnels
Ferme de l'Yonnière
GAEC du Pré Verger
61300 TORCHAMP - 02 33 30 84 76
Forget et Simonklein Associés

FERME DE L'YONNIÈRE
POIRÉ FERMIER

In 1999 terrible storms whipped through the Domfrontais region, hauling out trees young and old, offering the *poireculteurs* of the region a reminder of the power of nature. Yet Jérôme Forget at Ferme de l'Yonnière in Torchamp was not deterred. With no recent history of perrymaking in his family – like many, it had only been Calvados – when he arrived a few years before he immediately began planting trees to add to the ancient trees already there. And tall trees, so that cows could graze underneath, as is the norm. In 2000, he began again.

Now he has 10ha (25 acres) of perry pears and tall cider varieties. Self-taught, his passion is 'to conserve the process'. Walking with Jérôme and his partner Janice in the orchards at dusk is immensely calming. There are 30 varieties, including the region's flagship variety Plant de Blancs, alongside rarer varieties. A determined eco-warrior, Jérôme considers biodiversity as vital. 'For me the most important thing is that the fruit arrives naturally,' he says.

He was one of the band of producers to form the Domfront AOP, setting down standards for perry quality produced in the region. Yet this isn't the AOP *poiré* in my glass, magical though that is. Rather it's Poiré Fermier, his and business partner Justine Simonklein's farmhouse perry. That's because it's a perfect blend of light green tang and pear notes alongside tart tropical fruit flavours – unripe pineapple, papaya skin and starfruit. Almost water-white with an enthusiastic sparkle, it's off-dry, fragrant with pear notes throughout, plus the faintest herbal tinge.

There's 'nothing mathematical' about making perry, says Jérôme, 'not like cider. You never get the same quantities. It's always by instinct. *Très intéressant.*'

Issu de Vergers Traditionnels

region: Domfrontais, Normandy

fruit: primarily Plant de Blancs, with a blend of what else is ripe at that moment in time

life story: picked off the ground to ensure optimal ripeness – and because the vast trees are difficult to put a ladder against or to shake; gentle pressing, slow fermentation with natural yeasts

abv: 4.5%

if you like this: try Poiré Domfront AOP; Pyrus, Apéritif de Poire

experience: shop: Monday, Tuesday, Friday; phone ahead for guided tours; visit La Musée du Poiré, April–October

fermedelyonniere.com

CYRIL ZANGS
BRUT, 2016

region: Calvados, Normandy

fruit: a blend from 70 varieties, harvested by hand, October to mid-December

life story: apples stored by variety for up to six weeks to continue ripening; several rackings during six month fermentation; unfiltered cider bottled with no sulphites, stored horizontally up to three months; moved to A-frame for riddling; topped up with same cider

abv: 5%

if you like this: try This Side® Up; 2015; 2014; also Double Zéro, *eau de vie de cidre*; vinegars

experience: available in over 10 countries as well as France, see website for distributor details; follow social media for details of events

cidre2table.com

It's an Aladdin's cave, Cyril Zangs' cellar. Bottle cages are stacked high, plus what seems like oceans of A-frames, there for the twisting-and-tilting game known as riddling, to clear bottle-conditioned and bottle-fermented ciders and perries of their spent yeast.

Plus just enough room to sample a couple of Cyril's bottles with him.

Smiling and crowned with a black flat cap, Cyril's presence gives no indication of the late evening he'd had the night before. Busy times, visiting cidermakers from afar...

Initially attracted to the wine world, Cyril favours the natural approach. He was among the first to manually disgorge and his uncompromising philosophy extends to the end of the process. 'Why do they put sugar in?' he asks. 'I don't want my stomach to be the barrel.'

Apples, however, are a passion. There are 70 different varieties in his orchards. From the well knowns, like Douce Moën and Marie Ménard, through to lesser stars, like the aromatic Douce Normand and the late-harvesting, high-quality bittersweet Mettais. 'I prefer the later apples,' he says. 'The fermentation is slower.'

This is the 2016 vintage of Cyril's flagship brut cider. Yes, compared with 2015, it's a youngster, but the complexity is already beguiling. Rich amber in colour, this is a glorious celebration of the bittersweet cider apple. Unquestionably dry, there's incredible depth on the palate, including light caramel hints. There's the same fuzzy peach skin you find in the 2015 but this time it's enveloped by vivid fresh peach notes and warm apricot compote. The sparkle combines with dusky tannins to leave a long finish.

Definitely with a long life ahead, this will be fascinating to revisit.

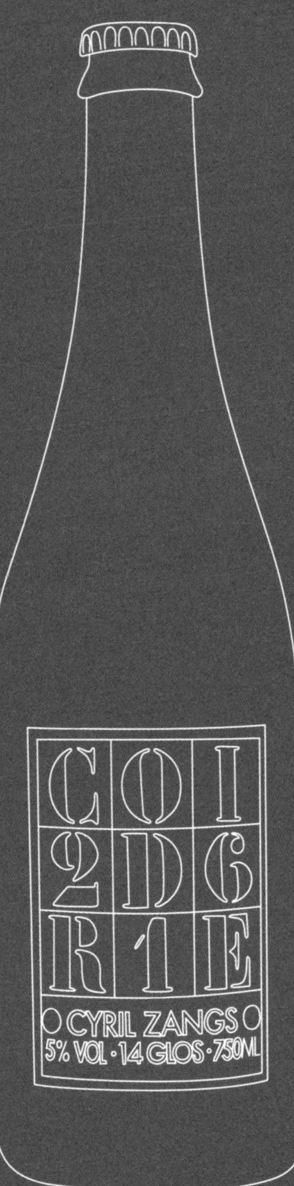
COI
2D6
R1E
CYRIL ZANGS
5% VOL · 14 GLOS · 750ML

FAMILLE
Dupont
CUVÉE
COLETTE
CIDRE
2015

FAMILLE DUPONT CUVÉE COLETTE, 2015

'In Pays d'Auge, they don't use too many sharp varieties. More bittersweet/sweet/bitter fruit. But here we prefer to bring something fresh and we use sharp varieties.' Mathieu Chevrier, sommelier at Domaine Dupont, is explaining the approach to cider of one of Normandy's leading Calvados producers, Famille Dupont.

'Cider is really important because we treat cider like a wine,' he says, before going on to tell me about how different varieties are fermented separately, first with natural yeast, and second using the traditional method, with champagne yeast.

Do they do use keeving? 'Of course!' he says. 'The *chapeau brun* is very important to bring a great flavour to the juice.'

The orchards are planted with cider in mind too. When the current head of the family, Jérôme, returned to the business in 1980, he planted trees, three rows of each variety. Along with the bitter Mettais, for example, and the bittersweet Bedan, came the tangy, fragrant Avrolles. In 2017, 5,000 more trees were planted, this time of just two key cider varieties, the bitter favourite, Kermerrien, and the sharp Petit Jaune.

And Petit Jaune is one of the two varieties in Cuvée Colette, the cider first produced by Jérôme's father, Étienne, when his mother Colette passed away.

Very fine bubbles stream through the glass, which is glinting pale gold. On the nose, ripe apples entice alongside slight cooked notes. On the palate, a variety show of flavours appears: tangy tart peach and apricot, ripe apples and green apples. Lemon and lime notes, mixed with orange zest to give a flavour that stays and stays.

It may not be the norm, but Dupont 'does' sharp pretty well.

region: Pays d'Auge, Normandy

fruit: sharp cider varieties Avrolles and Petit Jaune

life story: keeving, first fermentation to dryness at low temperatures for five to six months, natural yeast; champagne yeast added for second fermentation in bottle

abv: 7.5%

if you like this: try Cidre Réserve, aged for six months in ex-Calvados barrels; Cidre Bouché; Triple; Cidre Biologique

experience: visit the orchard and Cellar Door; check Facebook for forthcoming events

calvados-dupont.com

BORDATTO
TXALAPARTA, 2016

region: French Basque Country

fruit: regional varieties, Aphez Sagarra, Eztika, grown organically

life story: harvested and slowly fermented with natural yeast in a mix of oak barrels and stainless steel tanks; light, natural sparkle

abv: 7.5%

if you like this: try Basandere, nine-apple blend, bottle conditioned; Oreka, dry, still

experience: tasting tours during holidays, with local foods if pre-booked with a group; evening walks and live music in Bordatto bistro, July–Aug; available in Europe, Canada, Japan, Australia

domainebordatto.com

With a cider named Txalaparta, it's easy to see that Bixintxo and Pascale Aphaule are gazing more towards the Basque Country – their cidery, Bordatto, is only 56km (35 miles) from the Spanish border – than their Breton and Norman cousins.

Said to relate to the sounds of cidermakers crushing their apples, the *txalaparta* is the traditional Basque percussive 'instrument' – two musicians playing on wood – and the sound is often used to herald the arrival of the first ciders of the new season.

Txalaparta's back label also says *'vin de pomme'*, and sure enough, the cider shows wine-like structure instead of the rich warmth from up north.

With the perfect triangle of fruit, acid and light tannins, it's light gold in the glass, with light astringency. There's pineapple and fresh peach with beautiful, fuzzy tannins and fabulous fruit sweetness.

This is one of a diverse range crafted by Bordatto. Beginning life as a winemaker, Bixintxo decided the apple world held more excitement. He still grows vines but he devotes his energy to exploring how best to bring the most out of the local apples he champions.

Bixintxo grows 20 regional varieties and gathers in apples from nearby orchards. The trees he chooses are selected not because of their yields or when they can be harvested, but more because of their interesting aromas and flavours and the fact that they will survive in his organic, biodynamic environment.

'*Terroir* is often overlooked when people talk about cider, but I feel that characteristics of the site such as soil, orientation, tree age and varietal are just as important to cider as they are to wine,' he says. 'I want to prove it.'

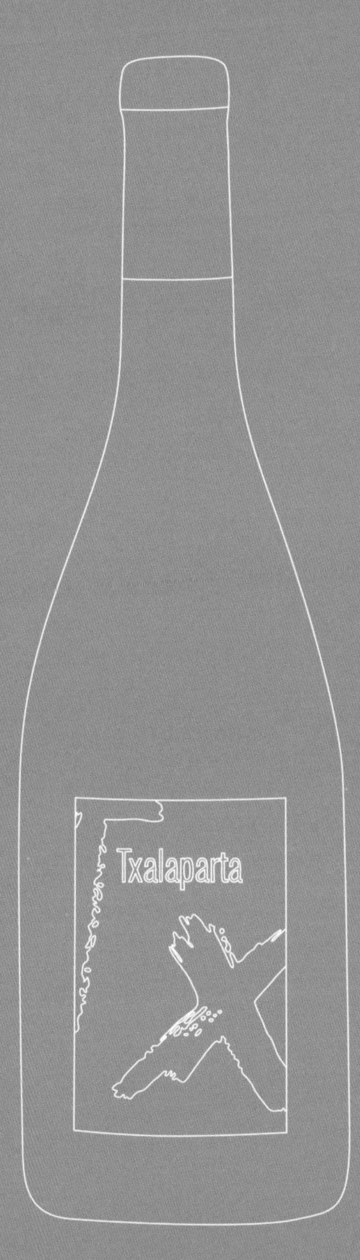
Txalaparta

SPAIN

Ever seen the Asturian cider pour? The dramatic, arm-held-aloft waterfall pour, channelling a vivid snappy cider laser-like into a tilted straight-sided tumbler? It's impressive. Imagine around 8,500 people doing this. That's the sight on Poniente Beach, Gijón in the last week of August, when the region's Natural Cider Festival each year sets a new Guinness World Record for simultaneous cider pouring.

Not just a bit of fun, it illustrates how embedded cider is in Asturian culture. This is the region that has recently applied for UNESCO World Heritage Status for its cider. Where the theatre of the pour, with the *escanciador* centre-stage, occurs everywhere – particularly in the friendly *sidrerías*.

Yet it hasn't always been so. Embattled after General Franco's attempts to wipe out Asturian identity, it took a plucky band of non-cidermakers in the 1990s to set up the Asturies XXI Foundation, dedicated to safeguarding the Asturian cidermaking culture.

Sidra de Asturias followed, in 2003, with a progressive quality agenda, regulating orchards as well as producers and co-operatives. Three official categories exist: *nueva expresión* and *natural espumosa*, but nothing beats a zesty *sidra natural*.

Falling mainly between historic Gijón and picturesque Villaviciosa, Asturian apple country is characterised by its mountainous Picos de Europa backdrop. With hundreds of indigenous apple varieties to draw from, Sidra de Asturias recently expanded its list of permitted varieties over threefold.

Whether it's modern or traditional, chances are that *sidra natural* is going to be tart and tangy. Of the 20 most popular apple varieties, sharp varieties account for over 90% of the trees planted. So what about the acetic notes often found in both Asturian and Basque

EXPLORE

Asturian Cider Region: lacomarcadelasidra.com

La Sidra, magazine of Asturies XXI Foundation: lasidra.es

Cider Museum of Asturias, Nava: museodelasidra.com

Natural Cider Festival, Nava Asturias, July

Natural Cider Festival, Gijón, Asturias, August

Villaviciosa Apple Festival, Asturias, October

The Land of Cider, includes Basque Cider Museum, the perfect place to start your visit; sagardoaren lurraldea.eus

The Day of New Cider, Sagardoaren Lurraldea, January

Basque Country Cider: euskal sagardoa.eus

Cider Day, Astigarraga, July

Apple Harvest Festival, Astigarraga, September

New season *txotx*, January–April

ciders? Regarded as a characteristic of the regions' distinctive production methods, providing these notes are not too intense, they are seen as a positive feature.

Next, head east to the hilly, verdant Basque Country. There you'll find hundreds of orchardists, dozens of cider houses and an unbeatable culture of marrying food and cider. Word has it that it was Basque fishermen who spread the cider gospel north up the French coast; whether true or not, records in the charming Basque Cider Museum in Astigarraga show the first written mention of apple tree orchards in the region to be as early as the 11th century.

Fast-forward to the middle of the 20th century and the scene doesn't look so good. With a stroke of genius, the *txotx* season was born. Celebrating the time when the 'new' season cider is ready, the majority of the region's cidermakers open their doors for four months from January. A universal but popular *txotx* menu is served, giving one and all a chance to taste the cider in the way that buyers of old used to do: fresh from the barrel.

More recently, Euskal Sagardoa was created, with its PDO scheme seeking to champion ciders made with apples from the Basque Country rather than bordering regions or countries. While 24 varieties account for 80% of the fruit, over 100 varieties are allowed. There's also a *premium* category, for those ciders scoring particularly highly in the Euskal Sagardoa tests. Plus *gorenak*, a quality-based category which allows apples from further afield to be involved.

Today the Spanish cidermakers face the challenge of raising the value perception associated with this artisanal product. What they have on their side are fiercely proud peoples, every one an eloquent advocate.

CASTAÑÓN
VAL DE BOIDES

Sidra Natural

region: Villaviciosa, Asturias

fruit: a blend of six or seven of the 76 apple varieties permitted by Sidra de Asturias PDO

life story: fermented in temperature-controlled chestnut barrels and stainless steel tanks for three months

abv: 6%

if you like this: try Sidra Natural; Castañón Brut

experience: choose between three levels of Guided Visits; watch Facebook for news of events, including SISGA, the Salón Internacional de les Sidres de Gala, September; plus festivals in Gijón, Nava, Oviedo and Villaviciosa

sidracastanon.com

It's not every day you get a sneak preview of a traditional-method sparkling cider ahead of release, hand-disgorged by the head of the family. But Julián Castañón isn't your average cider producer. Never afraid of doing things differently – check out his cider-vermouth, Roxmut, and the sweeter Xiz Frizzante too – Julián took the brave decision to invest in a beautiful, state-of-the art building for his new Cider Mill in 2011.

Drive down the entrance lane and be prepared for your spirits to soar. The dramatic elongated zigzag of the *lagar* roofline houses a modern stainless steel tank farm next door to a glorious barrel cellar, complete with vaulted ceilings and 20 chestnut barrels, each holding up to 18,000 litres (4,755 gallons).

Julián is the third generation to helm Castañón – coincidentally that's Spanish for chestnut. Initially, he wasn't sure if a life of cider was for him. Now he heads up the business, producing over a million litres (264,000 gallons) a year.

We are trying the Val de Boides, his *sidra natural*. It's a blend of a few of the region's favourites: the bitter semi-sharp Regona – Julián loves the aromas as well as the acids – and the semi-sharp Raxao, with a few lesser known heroes, including the aromatic Durona de Tresali and the sweet Ernestina.

Beautifully striking aromas of green fruits and apples mix with tart kiwi and grapefruit pith. Poured expertly by Julian, there's a good *pegue* (pronounced *perré)* and a long finish of citrus and Bramley apples. Julián suggests pairing it with grilled seabass with cider sauce, or crab.

So what does the future hold? Well, look out for that traditional-method cider. Well worth queuing for.

VAL D BOIDES
SIDRA
NATURAL

SIDRA DE ASTURIAS
DENOMINACIÓN DE ORIGEN PROTEGIDA
Villacubera
Tradicional
SIDRA NATURAL
14 meses
Maduración en bodega

CORTINA
VILLACUBERA TRADICIONAL

Celestino Cortina – 'Tino' to his friends – grew up in the family cider mill. Based in Amandi, just south of central Villaviciosa, for many the beating heart of Asturian cider culture, he recalls picking up apples before he started walking. But then he is the third generation in the cider business, and the cidermaking roots go back further than that.

Tino studied oenology for a few years before returning to the cider mill in his twenties. Involved ever since, he gets animated when he talks about the apples. Cortina has 10ha (25 acres) of orchards, but it's the hundreds of local farmers that Tino is particularly keen to discuss. 'Quality is more important than quantity,' he says. That rings true in the cidermaking too. Fermentation takes place at a lower temperature to preserve aromas, while 14 months of ageing for Villacubera enables the aromas to gain complexity, Tino explains.

Tasting the *sidra natural* straight from the stainless steel tanks, there are lovely yellow apple and light tangerine flavours alongside zesty green-apple notes. With the Villacubera itself, a fine white lacework of bubbles traces the inside of the glass. Zingy flavours of Granny Smith, Braeburn and unripe pineapple mix with zesty apple snow and slatey tannins.

We end up in Tino's 'tasting room', an atmospheric part of the cidery where a barrel with ciders sits alongside vintage relics, including a large wooden press and an old record book of apple deliveries, all the time flanked by a lengthy Sidra de Asturias banner detailing the region's key apples. Current president of Sidra de Asturias, the region's dynamic body that sets standards and governs quality, Tino manages to look to the future while respecting the past.

Sidra Natural

region: Villaviciosa, Asturias

fruit: a traditional mix of regional apples, as allowed by Sidra de Asturias

life story: after traditional fermentation, 14 months are spent ageing before release

abv: 6%

if you like this: try Villacubera Regona, 100% single varietal; Sidra de Hielo, award-winning ice cider

experience: take the Guided Tours, check website for details; visit Casa Cortina next door: Asturian gastronomy, warm welcome, and a menu that not only lists Cortina ciders but pictures the many apples that go into the blends

sidracortina.com

EL GOBERNADOR
ESPAÑAR

Sidra de Asturias

region: Villaviciosa, Asturias

fruit: three of the most popular Asturian varieties, bittersharp Regona plus sharps Raxao and Blanquina

life story: traditional pressing, temperature controlled fermentation, lengthy maturation, and bottling at low temperature to retain slight *pétillance*

abv: 6.5%

if you like this: try EM Brut Nature, traditional method

experience: Españar is in Denmark, The Netherlands, Sweden and Germany in Europe, and in the USA

sidraelgobernador.com

Two brothers, still in their twenties, decided to take on the cider world back in the 1990s. With experience gained at the El Faraón *sidrería* in the heart of Villaviciosa, El Gobernador was born. Over 20 years later, both Roberto and Francisco Martínez Sopeña are still at the helm and their cider company is one of the largest in the region.

Their key for quality is in the orchard – or orchards. The brothers have a number, each in a different microclimate, each bringing a different element to their ciders.

All three of the varieties for this cider are growing in the orchard in Viadi Tazones. Planted over a number of years, this also includes less popular varieties such as the bittersharp Meana and the tannic Clara.

Once harvested, the Martínez brothers adopt winemaking methods in their production, fermenting apple varieties separately. Modern presses and stainless steel tanks share space in the *lagar* with huge chestnut wooden casks on their characteristic pyramid-shaped *pegollos* (feet).

Españar means 'explosion' in Asturian, and that's what this is. Bright in the bottle, a riot of flavours opens up once it hits the glass – smashed green apples mixed with Cox flavours and ripe yellow notes, too. Finishing long, this falls into the *nueva expresión* style for Sidra de Asturias, for ciders that have been pressed and fermented traditionally, before being stabilised in some way, most generally filtered, to make them secure for both time and travel.

From 2015 to 2017, the brothers won the Best Orchard in Asturias award for their most recently planted orchard, San Justo, in recognition of the value they place on the importance of *terroir*.

SIDRA DE ASTURIAS

JR
SIDRA NATURAL
JR
ALTO INFANZÓN
www.sidrajr.es

JR
ALTOINFANZÓN TRADICIONAL

Imagine trekking on horse in the green hills and foothills of Asturias in the shadow of the Picos de Europa, stopping for refreshment at cideries along the way. That's Deva's Way in Alto del Infanzón, named after the region, the river and Deva, the ancient goddess of rivers and streams. Appropriately enough, one of the cideries along this route is JR, currently managed by Juan José Tomás Pidal, whose abiding passion is for the value of ancient, local apples.

Juan José grew up surrounded by cider. His uncle, his grandfather – it was everywhere. So no-one was surprised, least of all him, when aged 20 he began working with Amador Rodriguez. The last surviving member of JR's founding family, when Amador retired 15 years later, it was Juan José who became the manager.

While he likes to innovate, Juan José also believes fiercely in tradition, and the *lagar* plays a strong part in the community. There are just two ciders produced, the Tradicional, which we have here, and the Black Label, crafted with a more intense blend of Asturian varieties.

Fresh as a mountain stream on a warm day, the Tradicional's *espalmé* brings alive orange, yellow and green apple flavours. Beautifully textured and zesty with tart, stone-fruit flavours, there's a long finish. It's easy to see why this has won the all-important People's Prize at Gijón's Natural Cider Festival three times in the last 10 years.

Orchards remain as important as ever to Juan José, who has planted a few of his own. He applauds the official body, Sidra de Asturias, for widening the approved pool of cider varieties from 22 to 76 in 2017, but wants to go further. 'In my opinion there are still a few more to incorporate,' he says. 'I believe and I trust that this will happen in these next years.'

Sidra Natural

region: Cabueñes, Asturias

fruit: blend from 76 local varieties approved by Sidra de Asturias, supplemented with varieties from further afield if the harvest is poor

life story: temperature-controlled fermentation takes place in tanks, wooden, fibreglass or stainless steel

abv: 6%

if you like this: try the more complex JR Black Label

experience: follow Facebook for news of the many festivals JR is involved with, including concerts and SISGA; walk Deva's Way

sidrajr.es

MENÉNDEZ
VAL D'ORNÓN

Sidra Natural

region: Gijón, Asturias

fruit: four of the region's popular cider apples, Raxao, Regona, Durona and Collaos, as designated by Sidra de Asturias

life story: fermented in wooden chestnut casks over many months and bottled unfiltered

abv: 6%

if you like this: try Ecológica, new in 2018, made with organic apples

experience: visit La Montera Picona, Gijón; or Menéndez, guided tours by appointment, Monday–Saturday, excluding harvest-time, October–November; Natural Cider Festival, Gijón, August

sidramenendez.com

Menéndez is the house pour at Sidrería La Montera Picona, in Gijón. Located in an ordinary street in this busy cider-lover's city, be prepared for the hustle 'n' bustle of a market day whatever time you visit Emilio Rubio's friendly cider house.

When I arrived with my hosts, the gregarious crew behind *La Sidra* magazine and its parent cultural foundation, Asturies XXI, there was international football rattling away on the overhead screens, huge crabs in an aquarium in the centre (it's a specialist fish restaurant), and every table was taken.

Yet the sight you couldn't take your eyes off was the *escanciadores*, the skilled waiters pouring the *sidra natural* from an arm's height above their heads into traditional, straight-sided, broad-rimmed glasses. Whether behind the bar next to serried ranks of chilling bottles waiting for their turn or by the tables, the *escanciador* jet-streams the green-gold cider into a glass with solemn grace. With its lace-like *pegue* sparkling away, the glass is handed over with pride.

Each bar and restaurant chooses their *sidra* carefully. They visit and taste. Visit and taste. Some change each year, badging each one with their own name, others keep their favourite cider for years.

Emilio has two *sidras* from Menéndez; the standard and its PDO *sidra*, Val d'Ornón. The Val d'Ornón is electrifyingly zesty. The perfect livener while out and about and a suitable match to accompany a wide range of foods, particularly the local Asturian dishes.

Menéndez, for its part, spends much time spotlighting Asturian cuisine, forming alliances with cider houses such as la Montera.

Two Asturian passions united as one. Much like the cider house and its house pour.

SIDRA NATURAL
VAL D'ORNÓN
SIDRA DE ASTURIAS

RIESTRA

FUNDADA EN 1906
GUZMAN
RIESTRA
Sidra Brut Nature

GUZMAN RIESTRA
SIDRA BRUT NATURE, 2016

'I was born above the cider mill,' says Raúl Riestra with a laugh, when I ask about his first memories of apples. We are standing overlooking his sloping orchard of historic varieties right by the *lagar*. With their stooped demeanour and broadly splayed branches, they certainly look characterful.

The story has it that Raúl's great-grandfather Robustiano made his first press from a vast eucalyptus tree in 1907. The family moved to Sariego in the 1920s, and the current cidery, with its striking white walls and terracotta-tiled roof, was built in 1947.

Today, Raúl and his brother Rubén are in charge and there's a vibrant feel to the business. While Rubén looks after production, Raúl likes to travel, to check out the trends and to forge links with the likes of cideries such as Angry Orchard in the USA.

Sariego is almost midway between Gijón, Villaviciosa and Nava, and the limestone soils and altitudes between 300 and 800m (1,000 and 2,600ft) make for happy trees. Riestra has 5ha (12 acres) of its own trees and works with around 60 other orchardists.

Riestra introduced Brut Nature in 2012. 'I select the very best and most complex ciders for a good balance,' he says, describing the blend he crafts for the second fermentation. The haul of silverware since launch suggests this approach is working.

There's wonderful, fresh, tart apples on the nose alongside hints of hazelnuts, even caramel ice cream. The palate is beautifully dry and elegant, with tart exotic fruit and cooked apples. Raúl favours venison as a food match. Sassy bubbles make this a good aperitif and also, Raúl reckons, good with Cabrales, the distinctive local blue cheese. I'll have to try.

Natural Espumosa

region: Sariego, Asturias

fruit: primarily a blend of regional favourites, including Raxao, Blanquina and Carrió, plus some old varieties, some of which are unnamed

life story: traditional pressing and fermentation, with second fermentation in the bottle for eight months prior to disgorging

abv: 8%

if you like this: try Sidra Natural; Semi Seca; Sidra de Hielo

experience: check Facebook for news of festivals and events Riestra is involved with; find Riestra in USA, Canada, Denmark, The Netherlands, Romania, Lithuania

sidrariestra.com

TRABANCO
POMA ÁUREA, 2015

Brut Nature

region: Lavandera, Asturias

fruit: the two most popular Asturian cider varieties, Raxao and Regona

life story: slow, low temperature fermentation in vast chestnut barrels; a second fermentation in tanks adds the natural sparkle

abv: 6.5%

if you like this: try the renowned, refreshing black label Sidra Natural; Pecado del Paraíso

experience: choose your tour, orchard visit or tasting before heading into Casa Trabanco for lunch or dinner

sidratrabanco.com
casatrabanco.com

Samuel Trabanco recounts his first memory of apples – rather a dramatic one. He was five or six, jumping about on huge piles at harvest time, when they all fell on him. While that necessitated a rescue mission, over five decades later his respect and love for apples remain as strong as ever. 'It's the apple. If it doesn't arrive right, that is the main problem,' he says.

Samuel's favourite apples include the region's most popular, Raxao, a sharp variety, plus a few less famed ones. It's the red-streaked Raxao that is blended with the green, bittersharp Regona for Poma Áurea, Trabanco's *brut nature* cider.

There's a beautiful breadth to the aromas and flavours – yellow apples and fruits plus hints of orange zest as well as green apples. Undeniably dry, the bead of fine bubbles is lively and persistent.

Trabanco's substantial orchards provide most of its fruit. And it is still planting, including some rare varieties.

Trabanco has been in business since Samuel's grandfather Emilio founded the company in 1925, Samuel shares responsibilities with his siblings and cousins. His daughters already play key roles. Eva, a trained oenologist, is in charge of quality and new developments, running the lab with Trabanco's original oenologist, Jesús Gómez. Yolanda looks after Casa Trabanco, with its skilled *escanciadores* and regionally accented menu. Based in the village of Lavandera near Gijón overlooking hills and orchards, this is the site of the original cellar.

Samuel proudly shows me a picture of his young son, Samuel Junior, sitting with a broad smile on a mound of red and yellow apples. Like father, like son. Although hopefully without the tumble.

•19 25•
APPLE CIDER
POMA ÁUREA
BRUT NATURE
•SIDRA DE ASTURIAS•
DENOMINACIÓN DE ORIGEN PROTEGIDA

SIDRA NATURAL
SIDRERIA LA BALLERA
LA-BALLERA
Elaborado y embotellado por SIDRA VALLINA, S.L
PEON - VILLAVICIOSA - ASTURIAS - ESPAÑA

VALLINA FOR LA BALLERA SIDRA NATURAL

Cider and the apple are interwoven into the cultural fabric of Villaviciosa, the pretty coastal town set amid numerous orchards and *lagares*. This self-styled Capital of the Apple boasts apple-related sculptures as well as numerous friendly *sidrerías*. Its Natural Cider competition and the cider-pouring contest have acquired cult-like status.

'Guti' Rodriguez is another cultural icon. Guti has run La Ballera *sidrería* for over 20 years. Not just local, but national, fame for this cider house and seafood restaurant. Stars drop by for a chat and a *culín*, and a couple of years ago it was the location for Spain's much-heralded National Lottery Christmas advert.

Guti knows his natural cider. He judges the annual Escanciadores de Sidra – Cider Pourers – contest, and is president of the Sidra Casera, the home cidermaker association.

So what does Guti choose for La Ballera? When I visit, it's Vallina. Founded by Benjamín Vallina Cuesta in the 1950s, Vallina is now in the hands of son, Víctor. Winner of a number of awards itself, it focuses strongly on fruit selection.

Guti makes his selection the old-fashioned way, by visiting producers, tasting every barrel, identifying a few targets and following them on a weekly basis until he deems one of them ready. Then they're bottled and labelled specially for him.

The cider gleams golden in the glass. A characteristic acetic hint on the nose acts as a prelude to a zappy palate, full of green Granny Smith and starfruit. Beautiful tannins evolve to make this mouthwatering and lively.

When you visit, see if you can spot Guti in the mural behind the bar, depicting a fiesta in full flow. Friendly camaraderie with cider at its heart. Much like Villaviciosa itself.

region: Villaviciosa, Asturias

fruit: a blend of permitted Asturian varieties, chosen to ensure a good balance between tannins and freshness

life story: traditional pressing, natural yeast fermentation; first three months in chestnut barrels, next three months in fibreglass tanks to retain the natural sparkle

abv: 5.9%

if you like this: ask Guti about any other ciders he has or that he likes at the moment

experience: visit La Ballera, prop up the bar, enjoy the *croquetas*, soak up the atmosphere; check the festival calendar for the many apple- and cider-related fiestas

turismovilla viciosa.es

VIUDA D'ANGELÓN
PRAU MONGA, 2014

Brut Nature

region: Nava, Asturias

fruit: a blend, roughly equal proportions, of semi-sharp Perico, bitter semi-sharp Panquerina, sweet Verdialona and sharp Blanquina

life story: after pressing, a year in chestnut cask for the initial fermentation before spending two-and-a-half years in the bottle for secondary fermentation and further ageing

abv: 7.5%

if you like this: try Sidra Pomar Rosée, Sidra de Pera

experience: visit for guided tours and tasting, Tuesday and Thursday; check Facebook for events in Asturias, elsewhere in Europe and sometimes USA; Natural Cider Festival, Nava,

sidraviudaangelon pomar.es

'You won't be making a good product if you're not passionate.' That's Francisco Ordoñez Vigil explaining why, after studying oenology at university, he didn't head off to some smart vineyard to make wine. Admittedly, cider had been a family business for generations and there aren't any cidermaking courses in Spain. 'I got a chance to study to develop the cider heritage, which became almost like a hobby because I enjoy it so much.'

As you head round the *lagar* with Francisco, through the low-slung cellar packed with huge chestnut casks and then past dozens of A-frames with traditional-method cider in the middle of being riddled, that sense of enthusiasm is infectious.

Early memories for Francisco include smells of baked apples and apple juice – 'always the apple juice'. Today Viuda d'Angelón has 14ha (35 acres) of orchards in the apple haven near Nava, home of the region's Cider Museum of Asturias as well as its oldest cider festival.

Francisco uses wild yeast for the first fermentation, usually in an open tank followed by a barrel, and a specially selected house yeast for any secondary fermentations.

Viuda d'Angelón's range is extensive, including the distinctive Pomar Rosée sparkler. Made with a naturally red apple, it varies every year according to the vintage. Pale salmon in colour, in the vintage we tried it showed intriguing flavours of strawberries and vanilla.

Made with the traditional method, our cider here, the Prau Monga, has had over two years in the bottle before disgorging plus further time along the way, making it very well integrated with a beautiful texture. There's plenty of autumn apple fruits, hints of nuts and a lengthy finish. Definitely made with passion.

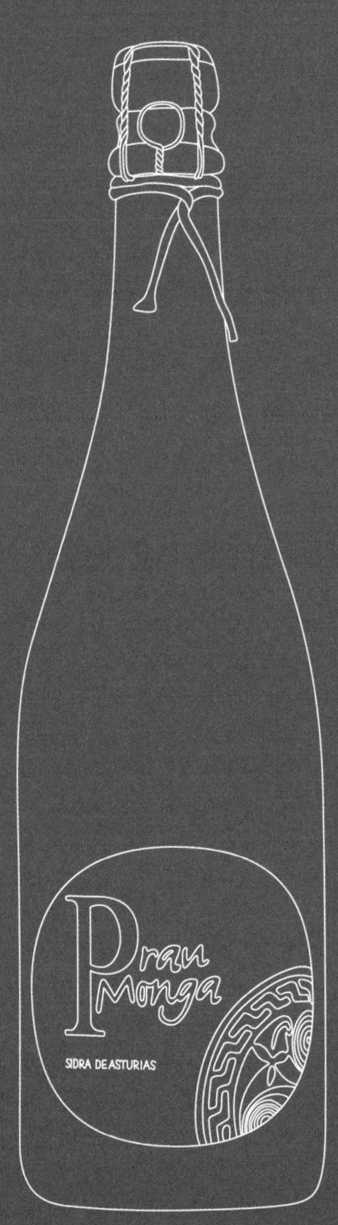
Prau
Monga
SIDRA DE ASTURIAS

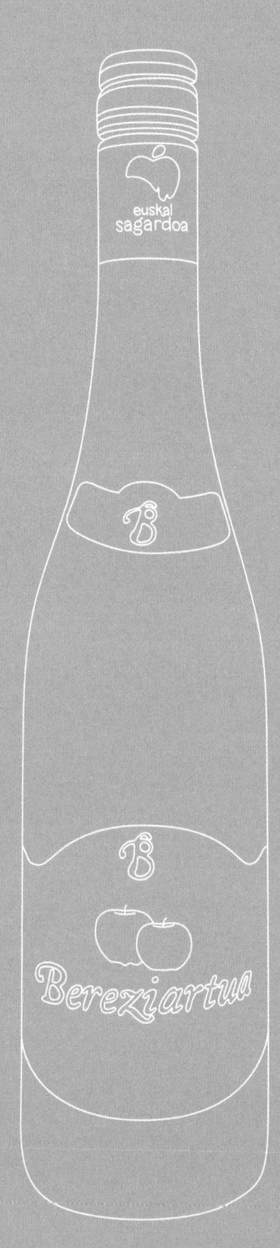
euskal
sagardoa
Bereziartua

BEREZIARTUA
SAGARDO NATURALA, 2017

Bereziartua, with its nearly 150 years of history, offers a hospitable welcome during the *txotx* season, between January and May. Based in Basque cider hotspot Astigarraga, the current helmsman is Joxe Miguel Bereziartua. With his trim moustache and upright stance, he has the *txotx* key tonight. During the rest of the year, sons Aitor and Oscar take care of sales and events, locally and throughout Spain, but for now they are in charge of the restaurant floor and kitchen, bringing out the traditional *txotx* dishes with a smile and a laugh. (The kids are playing peek-a-boo with Oscar, while his grill groans under the weight of giant T-bone steaks, a *txotx* menu highlight.)

But back to the cider. We're tasting the new vintage, arcing gracefully yet purposefully from the barrel into our glasses. We queue in a choreographed manoeuvre, waiting our turn to slip to the front for our glass to be filled – just one or two fingers' worth – before letting the next in line catch the cider stream, just like prospective buyers in the olden days used to.

Euskal Sagardoa, the new Basque Protected Designation of Origin scheme, is proudly emblazoned across some of the barrels, making it clear which barrels are destined for this shiny new quality denomination.

And that's what I've got in my glass now. Light yellow in colour with a tapestry of green apple and zesty flavours on the nose; much like Riesling this has both tang and bright fruit while remaining dry. With little evidence of tannins, a starfruit-like astringency offers a pleasurable grounding mouthfeel.

With the 2017 Euskal Sargardoa, the newest of its range, Bereziartua continues to look forward while treasuring the past.

Euskal Sagardoa

region: Astigarraga, Basque Country

fruit: special blend from the 25 most popular varieties in the Euskal Sagardoa approved list

life story: following milling and pressing, the juice is fermented in tanks, either stainless steel or vast wooden barrels, where the cider also ages for a while before bottling

abv: 6%

if you like this: try Bereziartua Original, Gourmet and Organic

experience: visit during *txotx* season, enjoy the traditional menu; contact the cidery to choose your tour and tasting

bereziartua sagardoa.com

GARTZIATEGI
SAGARDOA, 2017

Gorenak

region: Astigarraga, Basque Country

fruit: 75–85% Basque local varieties, with the rest from Galicia

life story: temperature controlled fermentation in stainless steel with natural yeast looking for that balance of 'acidity, bitterness and sweetness'

abv: 6%

if you like this: try the Euskal Sagardoa, made solely with Basque apples

experience: visit during *txotx* season, January–May; The Day of New Cider, Astigarraga, January; Santa Ana, Astigarraga, July; look for the season's opening event; follow Facebook for news of other events

gartziategi.com

It's the custom in the Basque Country to award a *txapela* – a beret, often black – to the winner. In fact, the word for champion is *txapelduna*, literally 'he or she who has the beret'.

Just like a silver cup gets engraved, in cider competitions these berets are embroidered, and it's not uncommon to see them proudly framed on *sagardoteki* walls around the Basque Country.

It's not often you see a wall with three families of *txapelas* displayed together. But this is Gartziategi, on the outskirts of Astigarraga, and they've been making cider for centuries.

Nere Lizeaga runs the cidery with her younger brother, Ander. 'It was our destiny,' she says of the move a few years back when they took the reins. 'We were always visiting our grandparents,' she explains.

Still both in their twenties, their great-grandfather, Joxe Mari, was one of the last to make vast barrels, the ones you can walk into, and there are a few of his creations still in the cellar, albeit lined with stainless steel these days. Rather than stick solely to chestnut, Joxe Mari preferred oak and acacia, because of the different flavours they impart to the cider.

But don't think Nere and Ander are stuck in the past. There are research projects with Friasoro, the local research lab, and the tank samples taste electrifying.

Strikingly slim, Nere shares her ciders with me. There are tart-green Bramley notes and ripe, warm Braeburn flavours with her Gorenak. Vivid Cox's Orange Pippin notes mix with hits of unripe exotic fruits and, buoyed by the acids and freshness, the length seems never-ending.

And the *txapelas*: Nere and Ander in 2015, her uncle in 2003, and her father in 1978. Now that's continuity.

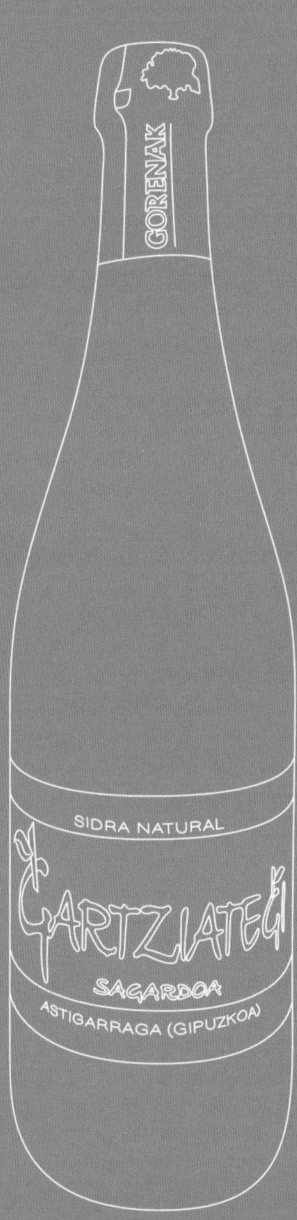
GORENAK
SIDRA NATURAL
GARTZIATEGI
SAGARDOA
ASTIGARRAGA (GIPUZKOA)

GORENAK
SACARDOA
SIDRA
GAZTAÑAGA
SAGARDOTEGIA

GAZTAÑAGA
SAGARDOA

'*Txotx*!' The call rings out. José Ángel Gaztañaga leads the way, *txotx* key in hand. Gaggles of lunchers get up from their benches, chatting animatedly as they follow José Ángel into his cellar to taste direct from the tanks. We were bang in the middle of *txotx* season and our time together was peppered with José Ángel darting up and down to perform the sampling ritual.

Before he set up Gaztañaga in the late 1980s, José Ángel had been a keen home cidermaker. For a while he ran cidermaking alongside his 'proper' job, at the Michelin factory, but he had always had the idea of a *sidrería* so, when the chance arose, cider took over.

Among the pioneers of stainless steel tanks, José Ángel wants his ciders to be produced as naturally as possible. No sulphites for the last eight years, his string of wins at various regional competitions show his style is appreciated, and the cellar walls littered with winning *txapelas* offer ample evidence.

Today the *sagardotegi* is a family affair, with the next generation, Axier, involved as well as José Ángel's brother and wife. The majority of the fruit comes from 15 nearby farms.

We have his Gorenak in the glass. Pale yellow sun in colour, the nose smells like yellow melon flesh. Flavours of Granny Smith and kiwi fruit mix with the zest of Bramleys. Elegant and refreshing, this is multi-layered with a long finish, working well with the *txotx* menu. Speaking of which, it will soon be time for the next *txotx*. Best get ready.

Gorenak

region: Andoain, Basque Country

fruit: blend of mainly local Basque apples

life story: Initial blends are made up prior to fermentation once the juice has been analysed after pressing; natural fermentation in stainless steel

abv: 6%

if you like this: try Gartziategi Gorenak

experience: Gaztañaga's *txotx* season runs January–May; see the traditional dancing on opening night; restaurant open all year

sidreriagaztanaga.com

ISASTEGI
SAGARDO NATURALA

Euskal Sagardoa

region: Tolosa, Basque Country

fruit: special blend, primarily seven or eight varieties, including the sharp variety, Errezil, cherished for its enchanting aromas

life story: after crushing; the juice is fermented through to dryness in stainless steel and plastic tanks; aged until bottling or the *txotx* season

abv: 6%

if you like this: try the Gorenak

experience: visit during *txotx* season; one of the most popular *sagardoteki*, take advantage of bus services from Tolosa to reach your hillside destination

isastegi.com

Based less than an hour outside of Astigarraga, Isastegi nestles among the picturesque foothills of Mount Intxurre, gazing towards Mounts Ernio and Aralar. With the perfect microclimate for apples, trees are low-slung to aid hillside harvesting. Where once livestock grazed, Isastegi grows 10 varieties of apples.

For Isastegi, it was the downturn of farming fortunes in the 1980s that persuaded Miguel Mari and Lourdes Lasa to move into cider full time. They had always made cider – every farmer did – but this was going to be different.

And so it was. Before long, the quality was noticed and a decade later they began producing cider for the Eroski supermarket group. Isastegi was also among the first Basque ciders to reach the USA.

Today, beautifully whitewashed buildings house both the cellar and the *sagardoteki*. The hillside location means gravity lets streams of apples roll down to the mills. Fermentation takes place with natural yeast in stainless steel, and there's an overwhelming feeling of freshness that flows into the glass.

A vivid rush of Bramley apple notes mixes with apple snow on the nose with a hint of tangerine zest. In the mouth, it's dry and tangy, with Cox and pear notes leading into a long, tart, green finish, and an astringency that lingers.

Our host for our visit, Joseba Lasa, is the latest family member to join the business. With oenology training on top of his physics degree, he's busily learning everything. He's already looking forward to trying new ideas, and proudly shows us his latest cellar purchase – a mini stainless steel tank, perfect for trial batches. The next chapter is about to begin.

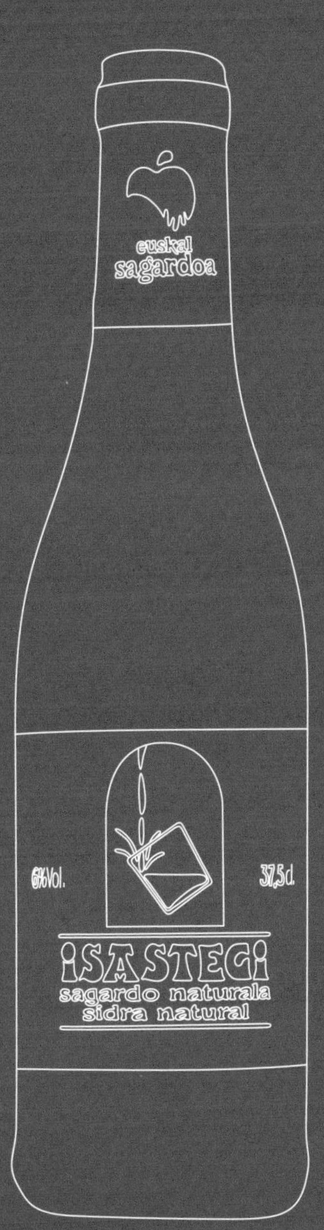
euskal
sagardoa
6% Vol.
37,5 cl.
ISASTEGI
sagardo naturala
sidra natural

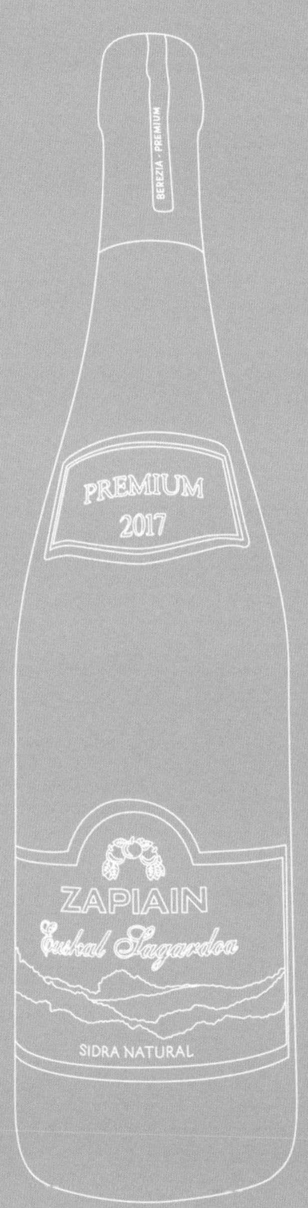
BEREZIA - PREMIUM
PREMIUM
2017
ZAPIAIN
Euskal Sagardoa
SIDRA NATURAL

ZAPIAIN
PREMIUM, 2017

It might have been sunny outside with the bright blue sky of spring, but Egoitz Zapiain was in his cobalt-blue puffa with its red zip as we descended into the cool of the Zapiain cellar. Dwarfed by the vast chestnut *kupelas*, each holding tens of thousands of litres, he explained how he had chosen work in Bordeaux, Irouléguy and Rioja Alavesa, selecting wineries where aromatic wines were favoured. And it's these intense aromas we had just experienced in his stainless steel tanks. Starfruit, pineapple and other yellow-fruit notes, plus a little hint of green still peeping out from some electrifying young ciders.

Bringing a winemaker's sensibility into the cellar, Egoitz ferments each style of apple separately. Where he's preserving the aromas, it will be a slightly lower temperature; where it's the tannins, a little warmer.

After fermentation, the ciders move to the barrel cellar, letting nature take over for maturation and clarification. Each will taste different – the one we try has white and yellow melon notes.

At the end of our cellar journey, we try the bottled Premium Euskal Sagardoa cuvée from 2017. That freshness and vivacity is still present. Apple snow and hits of tangerine wake up the apple. Zesty green acids give a long finish while ripe green fruit flavours shine through.

The Zapiains have 18ha (45 acres) of their own orchards and draw on over four times that from dozens of local farmers. They have been in cider forever – there's a reference back to the late 16th century. Yet the passion is undimmed. At just 36, Egoitz has already spent half his life in the business, and his cousin Jon is similarly involved. The future's looking strong.

Euskal Sagardoa

region: Astigarraga, Basque Country

fruit: honed blends of apples from Astigarraga, Tolosa and Errezil, evolving as the harvest season progresses

life story: seven-day fermentation in stainless steel; maturation for up to six months in *kupelas* before bottling

abv: 6%

if you like this: try the Euskal Sagardoa; for something surprising, try Bizi-Goxo, dessert cider crafted from Errezil variety, either via apples freezing on the tree in cold years, or by freezing the juice

experience: visit during *txotx* season; Cider Day (*Sagardo Eguna*), Astigarraga, July; check Facebook for other events

zapiain.eus

ZELAIA
SAGARDO NATURALA, 2017

Gorenak

region: Hernani, Basque Country

fruit: primarily local cider varieties, including from their own orchards, topped up as necessary from further afield

life story: Basque apple varieties, roughly half of which are sharp varieties, fermented with temperature control, aged for three months in huge barrels

abv: 6%

if you like this: look out for special bottlings, such as the María de Labayen, named in honour of a feisty female cidermaker from the 16th century

experience: visit during *txotx* season for a truly atmospheric evening; perhaps, as is the Basque way, there'll be an outburst of glorious song, as when I was there

zelaia.es

Tasting Zelaia's Sagardo Naturala makes you realise why the region is so strongly wedded to drinking these ciders as fresh as possible. With a fragrance of meadow flowers, almonds and kiwi fruit, it's electrifying on the palate, wrapping up beautiful Granny Smith and Cox apple notes with pears and starfruit, plus pineapple, tart melon and orange zest.

Maialen Gaincerain, one of three sisters at the helm, relates how they try to pick the apples just before they reach full ripeness. There's less risk of oxidation, she says, and more chance of the green apple freshness they are after.

Independent thinking obviously runs in the family. It was Maialen's father, José Antonio who, with his wife Nati, defied his own father's worries to move the farm's focus from a mixed model to cider. Since then, growth has been steady and, in 2013, José Antonio handed the reins over to the youthful sisters, Maialen, Oihana and Jaoine.

Maialen is in charge of production, Oihana looks after oenology, while Jaoine has marketing and finance in her hands. All three lend a hand throughout the all-important *txotx* season, just as they did when they were young and their father fired up the barbecue for his guests.

In 2009 they joined with Zapiain to plant 7ha (17 acres) of orchard in neighbouring Navarra, including many local varieties. For her part, Maialen has a few favourites, including the acid/bittersweet Urtebi Txiki ('it's easy to harvest'), acid/sweet-sour Goikoetxea, for its flavour, and the tannic Moko, determinedly biennial but, when it arrives, 'strong and colourful'.

Much like the cidery itself then.

GOKENAK
2017
Sagardo naturala
Zelaia
Sidra natural

Ribela
www.ribela.es
SIDRA
Maceiras Vellas
Producto de Galicia

RIBELA
MACEIRAS VELLAS

When Jesús Armenteros and his family and friends set up Ribela back in 2013 they were seen as 'crazies'. How things have changed. Now they are respected and admired, but back then, there were no commercial cidermakers of note based in Galicia. Sure, there's a history of apple growing, 400 varieties are indigenous to Galicia, and cidermaking stretches back millennia. But when Galician wine came of age, cider lost its way. What apples were grown were shipped off to Asturias or the Basque Country.

Step in Jesús. With several decades of hobby cidermaking under his belt, plus inspiration from other cidermaking cultures, including Brittany, Normandy and the USA, he and his family took the plunge.

'We set Ribela up because of tradition, love for the countryside, sustainable farming and as a tribute to our ancestors as well as the possibility of turning our hobby into a business,' says Jesús.

Starting with 2ha (5 acres), soon demand meant they partnered with other orchardists, particularly in their quest for highly prized apples such as Rabiosa or Raiada.

These apples are among those in Maceiras Vellas. Named in honour of the old trees from whence they came, Jesús regards this as the most elegant of his ciders.

There's plentiful aromas of rich, ripe autumnal apples and warm summer flowers, plus green apple notes. Orchard fruit salad, bruised apple notes and ripe pineapple flavours play alongside a snappy twang of acidity and relatively soft tannins.

'Our project is based on communicating our history through our different varieties of apple, our land and our climate, producing a cider in a craft way which is highly valued'. The world is richer for this.

region: Estrada, Galicia

fruit: blend of indigenous apples including Marafonsa, Freixerana, Pimienta or Ollo Mouro with Rabiosa and Raiada from the region's oldest trees, mostly over 60 years old

life story: natural yeast fermentation, for 30–45 days; aged further in stainless steel where malolactic fermentation takes place; slight carbonation adds to the natural sparkle

abv: 5.5%

if you like this: try Besta, Spain's first hopped cider, with Cascade and Citra

experience: visit the *lagar*, contact beforehand; check Facebook for opening hours; find Ribela in Portugal, Italy, USA and Canada

ribela.es

GERMANY, ITALY & ELSEWHERE IN EUROPE

Eight countries, 13 ciders. From 3% to 10% alcohol. From a region where *apfelwein* has charge of an entire sector of a wine-adoring nation to several countries where our featured producers are the first to commercialise craft ciders, from majestic perry pear trees to orchards within sight of the Matterhorn. This chapter is arguably the most diverse. A true harlequin selection of cider and perry styles.

Here, there is no common historical or geographical thread. Culturally speaking, the only similarity is the unremitting passion shown by our producers.

Despite having its own world-renowned wine culture, **Germany** also boasts a variety of cider styles. Heading these is the sassy *apfelwein*, crafted from dessert and cooking apples and served up in *bembels* (homely blue-and-white ceramic jugs) in the busy Sachsenhausen district of Frankfurt.

Also known as *viez* towards the French border, there is a 150-km (110-mile) Viezstrasse, or Route de Cidre, which winds through orchards nestling under mountain ridges and in river valleys.

Rich soils in Hesse afford eco-pioneers like Andreas Schneider a varied apple and pear palate with which

EXPLORE

Apfelwein: apfelwein.de

The Cider Route, Austria: moststrasse.mostviertel.at

Cider World, Frankfurt, April: cider-world.com

Cider from Poland: ciderfrompoland.com

Cider Day: mostviertel.at/tag-des-mostes

Rigtig Cider, Copenhagen, August: rigtigcider.dk

Slavnost Cideru, Prague, June: slavnostcideru.cz

Cider Explorer, Natalia Wszelaki: ciderexplorer.wordpress.com

to work. Meanwhile, Jörg Geiger seeks to rescue 'meadowfruit', the historic pear and apple varieties of the region. Tuning into Central Europe's swathe of perry orchards, we find Hans-Jörg Wilhelm at Hohenloher, with his Tribun Extra Brut crafted with fruit from just one tree.

The tiny principality of **Luxembourg** offers ancient orchard backdrops. We focus on the unheralded aromatic gem, Erbachhofer. Rare varieties emerge once more in **Switzerland** with Cidrerie du Vulcain, although here it is rescued apple, pear and quince that go into the press.

Head to the **Italian** border for another apple saviour. Gianluca Telloli crafts ciders with fruit from unloved trees within sight of the Matterhorn, while further east, Floribunda in the South Tyrol produces some of the most aromatic ciders I've ever encountered.

Austria boasts pear and apple cultures, with *most* being the term for both cider and perry. Moststrasse and Tag des Mostes celebrate the rich seam of pears in the region, and there's even a town named after them, Mostviertel. We head to the European apple belt in Styria, however, to meet Austria's first hopped cider specialist, Blakstoc.

Next our European tour takes us to the northern half of **Sweden**. Not only is Brännland producing ice cider in the Québécois way – winter rather than a chiller responsible for freezing the juice – they are also planting hardy apples in northerly orchards.

Poland grows over two million tonnes of apples each year, primarily regular dessert varieties. But that's not for the Wiechowskis and Kwaśne Jabłko. As well as homing in on indigenous varieties, they have planted 160 north-east European apple varieties, plus 20 varieties from Britain.

Finally our Grand Tour takes us to Pärnumaa in south-western **Estonia**, where the Roosimaas welcome us into an orchard with local varieties, including Talvenauding, a variety regarded as the Kingston Black of Estonia. This is truly the rainbow chapter of the book.

SCHNEIDER
BOSKOOP ALTE BÄUME 53, 2016

Mit echtem Speierling

region: Frankfurt, Germany

fruit: the heritage Boskoop apple, from trees over 50 years old, with Speierling added to bolster tannins

life story: harvested by hand; natural fermentation; pomace used as compost for the trees

abv: 4%

if you like this: try Boskoop; Goldrenette mit Mispel; Goldparmäne mit Weinbirne

experience: visit the Cider Inn, Farm Shop, events; sponsor a tree; check website for details

obsthof-am-steinberg.de

'We let nature run wild,' says Andreas Schneider, the pony-tailed eco-warrior behind Obsthof am Steinberg. And, with a policy of making up to 50 different ciders and perries each year, simply naming them with a number when the juice arrives in the fermentation hall, you can see what Andreas means.

Andreas is the second generation at the helm of Obstof am Steinberg. He took over in the early 1990s, switching to organic production the following year. Today his 16ha (40 acres) of fruit includes 250 different varieties, nearly half of which are apples. The focus is on old varieties and not rushing any stage, whether it's in the orchard or the cidery. Success is reflected in receiving not one but three Pomme d'Or awards over the last decade at the Frankfurt Cider World competition.

Located just 15km (9 miles) north of Frankfurt, gentle breezes help Obsthof am Steinberg's organic quest, and the soils draw on riches laid down in the last ice age.

One of the most popular apples in Central Europe, Boskoop originally arrived in The Netherlands from France in the mid-19th century. Fragrant with good sugars and acids, Boskoop has few tannins. So Speierling, a Mediterranean fruit, is added. An endangered species in its own right, Andreas grows a number of different varieties to encourage its survival.

Light gold in the glass, the nose is complex and intense with notes of apricots and tangerine zest. These flavours join ripe, exotic apple flavours on the palate. Medium sweet with light tannins, there's just enough acidity to balance herbal notes.

Just as his parents gave Andreas a natural playground in which to learn, so he shares the delights of his farm with those who want to enjoy this eco-friendly haven.

schneider
53
BOSKOOP ALTE BÄUME
mit echtem Speierling
2016
www.obsthof-am-steinberg.de

Weidmann
&Groh
2015er
SPEIERLING

WEIDMANN & GROH
SPEIERLING, 2015

While Weidmann & Groh may be best known for their spirits, cider and perry also play an important part in this family-run producer in Hesse.

With 5ha (12 acres) of orchards, growing everything from apples to cherries, quality rather than quantity is the quest. It all began some 30 years ago, when Reiner Weidmann began selling his fruit brandy. Two decades later, having served a two-year distilling apprenticeship elsewhere, son-in-law Norman Groh joined with Robert, and Weidmann & Groh was born.

With its base in Ockstadt, Friedberg, less than an hour north of Frankfurt, cider and perry have been part of the commercial picture for a decade – Norman had been involved with orchards since his teens. The orchards are a familiar sight in the lush region of Wetterau, known for its fertile soil. Whether destined for distilling or for the cider/perry route, the team waits for perfect ripeness before harvesting.

Speierling, the magic ingredient that adds a dash of astringency to balance the sweetness and acids, is itself an ancient fruit. A member of the rowan tree family, it is cited by Plato and the Babylonian Talmud.

Once harvested, the Speierling is pressed and the juice cold-stored until needed.

Still and, like several of the Weidmann & Groh ciders, with an almost wine-like approach, this is rather different. Off-dry in sweetness and watery yellow in colour, it is distinctly aromatic with a long finish. The palate is bright, with yellow, ripe, bruised fruit flavours, and lemony/orange notes on the finish. To ensure the full fragrance, don't serve too warm.

Today, Norman's brother Lorenz has joined the team, along with the newest addition to the range – Kultland beer brewed with barley from the Wetterau region. Versatility and provenance arm-in-arm.

Apfelwein mit Speierling

region: Friedberg, Germany

fruit: local apple blend with Speierling, the ancient Mediterranean fruit dating back to Ancient Greece

life story: once the fruit is ripe, both apple and Speierling trees are shaken and the fruit collected from tarpaulins placed below

abv: 6.5%

if you like this: try Boskop, the cider awarded Best in Show at the 2017 Sagardo Forum, Astigarraga; Kaiser Wilhelm; Goldparmäne

experience: find Weidmann & Groh in restaurants like Lorsbacher Thal in Frankfurt

weidmann-groh.de

APFELUNDWEIN
ONTARIO, 2014

region: Hesse, Germany

fruit: Ontario, a late-harvest, multi-purpose apple, used in the past in place of lemon for its citric-like qualities

life story: late harvest; fermentation using cultured yeast; juice is chaptalised to raise the abv; secondary fermentation in the bottle, followed by *dosage*

abv: 10%

if you like this: try Apfelundwein's range of still, single-varietal *apfelweins*

experience: arrange a cider tasting in the shop; choose the food pairing option to try local dishes, including boiled potatoes with green sauce, and *handkäse mit musik*, 'hand cheese with music'

apfelundwein.de

An apple with an interesting history provided the fruit for the winner of the 2018 Cider World Sparkling Cider/Apfelwein category as Ingrid and Wulf Schneider's Apfel-Vino took the trophy with their Ontario Topp-Secco.

Ontario was created in – you guessed it – Ontario, Canada, in the early 19th century from a cross between two New York apples: the relatively sweet, crisp Wagener, once popular in the markets of the US and the UK, and the already popular, more intense Northern Spy. The result, more of an all-rounder, travelled back to Europe and resettled mainly in Germany, where, according to the Schneiders, it can be found in 'almost all rural gardens'.

While its lemony notes made it a fine citrus substitute for some, for the Schneiders it's ideal for their traditional-method sparkling wines because of its high acidity alongside an intense flavour profile.

Pale straw in the glass with elegant bubbles, and some autolytic notes, the palate is floral with peach, apricot and ripe, yellow apple flavours. Wine-like, with a great acid balance.

A boutique producer, the couple began 10 years ago when Wulf took early retirement in his mid-50s from his engineering career. Having grown up amid the forests, Wulf wanted to get back to nature. Sustainability and heritage varieties are important, new orchards have been planted, and production has grown to 10,000 bottles, split between still and sparkling. 'What is ripening in the apple you should taste in the *apfelwein*,' they say. No worries there, then.

APFEL - SELEKTION
TOPP-SECCO
ONTARIO 2014

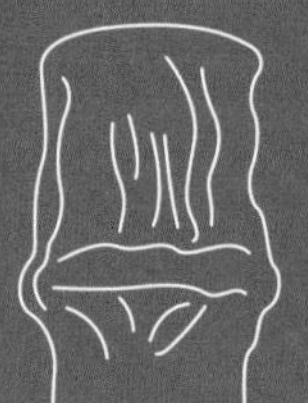
HOHENLOHER
TRIBUN
Birnenschaumwein
2015
extra brut

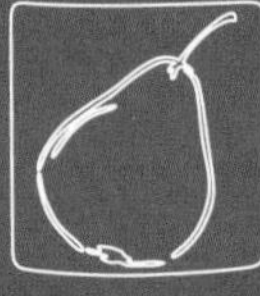
Handgerüttelt · traditionelle Flaschengärung
Erzeugerabfüllung Hans-Jörg Wilhelm

HOHENLOHER
TRIBUN, 2015

Pony-tailed and Panama-hatted, Hans-Jörg Wilhelm is the philosopher ciderist. 'It started out of a hobby,' he tells me, having explained how the local culture where he lived meant that everyone used to make cider in their basements.

Hans-Jörg has 240 trees, many of which are old and several of which reach 40m (130ft) in height. If his Pyrus perry is where it all began, with all its delicate pear snow flavours and elegant sparkle, Tribun is where things get serious.

Made from the Romelder pear, with only one tree, just 240 bottles are crafted each harvest. Not many people work with this pear because of its high acidity. Hans-Jörg likes Romelder, but only after it's had 24 months in bottle. 'It takes more time to have success with the aroma,' he says.

This time gives depth and a dryness that both delineate and define the flavours. Palest water-white in the glass, white melon and pear rub alongside light hazelnut notes on the palate, while a fine sparkle leads to a long finish.

Things are done organically and, where possible, biodynamically. 'I'm always looking at the earth,' he says. Nature can be cruel though. Being in a valley, frost can hit hard. In 2017, frost around blossom time devastated his crop completely. Luckily 2018 is looking good as I write.

While his cider house is nearby, where Hans-Jörg lives just happens to sit upon the ancient crypt of Unterregenbach. Dating back over 1,000 years, this was once one of the biggest churches in Europe. Hans-Jörg delights in sharing his archeological passion with visitors, and has even married cider and history together for some of his tours and visits. Now that's true culture.

region: Baden, Germany

fruit: the Romelder pear, aka Riesling pear

life story: cool fermentation for two to three months with champagne yeast; traditional fermentation, 24 months in the bottle, zero *dosage* at disgorging

abv: 8%

if you like this: try Hohenloher Pyrus; Campano Qui Quince

experience: visit the farm shop on Thursdays; check Events tab for outside appearances; mix cider with an archeology or biodynamic garden tour; hike with Hans-Jörg

hohenloher-schaumweine.de

JÖRG GEIGER
CRAFT CIDER, SCHWÄBISCHER

region: Swabia, Bavaria, Germany

fruit: MeadowFruit blend of regional varieties, roughly two-thirds apple to one-third pear

life story: after harvest, fruit is matured further for a few weeks before milling to enhance aromas and tannins; cold fermentation takes place in tank

abv: 3.5%

if you like this: try Bratbirne Brut, sparkling pear wine; Eisapfel, a rarity; Hauxapfel, aged in *barriques*

experience: check out Visit Jörg Geiger tab on website: guided tours and workshops; visit Gasthof Lamm; check out the Events section on the website

manufaktur-joerg-geiger.de; lamm-schlat.de

The Swabian Alb may look picturesque and placid, but modern ways are endangering some of nature's most majestic beings. Coming from the time when sheep and sometimes cows grazed underneath, the tall, graceful apple and pear trees have been feeling unloved and unwanted. Enter stage left Jörg Geiger, a chef with generations of roots in the region – his family have owned the popular Gasthof Lamm in the small town of Schlat since the 17th century.

While hundreds of local growers were donating their apples and pears to the distillery underneath Gasthof Lamm, Jörg felt this wasn't enough. Not everyone wanted to drink spirits, he reasoned, so why not make cider and perry? First though, he needed to secure the future of the trees that bore his beloved fruit.

He championed the Champagner Bratbirne pear, probably one of the oldest native pears, securing its place on the Slow Food International Ark of Taste list. He established the MeadowFruit Association which, with Slow Food Germany, takes care of a selection of historic pear and apple trees, including the Bratbirne, and another of his favourites, the Stuttgarter Gaishirtle MeadowFruit Pear. This is a small pear, also known as honey or sugar pear, the name allegedly stemming from the goat herder (Gaishirtle) who discovered it.

But this is a cider, so why all the pears? 'The tradition in our area is always to blend apple and pear wine [cider],' says Jörg. Medium-light on the palate, there are hints of vibrant pear throughout, as well as apple snow and fresh apple flavours. With a citrus hint on the finish, the sparkle is well judged, adding piquancy to the experience.

While the battle to save the trees is still ongoing, the prospects are certainly looking better.

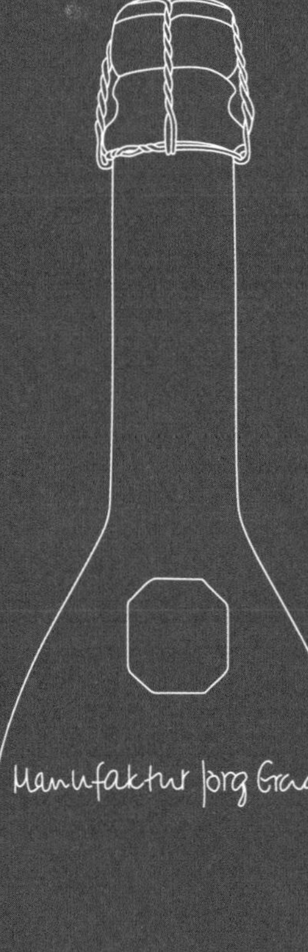
Manufaktur Jörg Geiger

Manufaktur Jörg Geiger
Craft Cider
SCHWÄBISCHES WIESENOBST
SCHWÄBISCHER CIDER MILD FRUCHTIG
Handverlesene Wiesenäpfel | Weinbirnen

Maley
CIDRE
DU SAINT BERNARD

MALEY
CIDRE DU SAINT BERNARD, 2017

'Why am I making cider? I am a winemaker. It's the patrimony, the *terroir* – the potential is enormous and the possibilities are endless.'

This is Gianluca Telloli speaking from the Alps. The views include the Matterhorn and historic amphitheatres. His cidery, Maley, straddles the Italian and French borders, and uses apples from both the Aosta and Chamonix Valleys. Two countries now, but go back 160 years and it was one, the Kingdom of Savoy, with its own cider culture. Then came division. Then devastation: Mussolini declared cider too 'French'. Drinks under 7% were made illegal.

So when Gianluca, a talented oenologist born in the mountains, fell upon graceful, untouched 100-year-old trees, he determined to change things. Today, up in the mountains, between 600m (2,000ft) and 1450m (4,750ft), he nurtures 10 ancient apple and pear varieties, and is always on the look-out for more trees.

'I believe that cider deserves the dignity of great wines,' he tells me. 'We work with this logic and try to bottle the freshness of our mountains and the minerality of the rocks.'

It's that laser-like precision and exquisite orchard notes that strike me when I first taste Maley's Matterhorn cuvée, thanks to Mark Gleonec, international judge and president of Cornouaille PDO. Today it's the off-dry Saint Bernard in my glass. The palate is perfectly poised, with peach-ripe notes and cooked apricot alongside apple and pear notes and amazing freshness.

'When you look upwards at the top of the world, it gives you a huge opportunity to really appreciate your territory.' With Gianluca's help, we all have a chance to share in his vision.

region: Aosta, Italy

fruit: ancient apples: Raventze, Reinette, Groin de Veau, Croison de Boussy, Petit Jaune; pear: Blesson, for aroma, structure and sweet tannins

life story: made using the *ancestrale* or *pét-nat* method, whereby the cider is bottled before fermentation has finished, building up natural sparkle

abv: 3%

if you like this: seek out Matterhorn or Jorasses; try Cristallier, Maley's cider vermouth, with 25 herbs

experience: watch sabrage on the website; contact Gianluca to arrange visit; look for Maley at Alajmo restaurants, Italy, and others, including Hôtel Belles Rives, Cap d'Antibes, France

maleymontblanc.com

FLORIBUNDA
APFEL CIDER ALLA MELA, 2017

region: South Tyrol, Italy

fruit: dessert apple varieties, Topaz, Pilot, GoldRush

life story: hand-picked ripe apples wait two weeks before milling and pressing; natural fermentation before secondary fermentation in the bottle

abv: 6%

if you like this: try the perfumed Quince cider; Elderflower cider, crafted with addition of homemade elderflower 'champagne'

experience: Japan is Floribunda's biggest customer; with prior warning, the Eggers welcome visitors; ciders are available in local organic shops and the hotel Preidle Hof; biosudtirol.com for organic farming holidays

floribunda.it

'My first memories?' Magdalena Egger laughs gaily. She recounts tales of helping her father, Franz, at harvest, not just collecting apples off the ground but climbing up into the tree and throwing the apples down from on high.

Nearly 20 years later, they are both still involved. She's helping out when not immersed in her agriculture degree, and Franz is responsible for some of the most fragrant ciders I've encountered. And all this from a region – South Tyrol – which is famous in Italy for apples but where wine is King, Queen and Jack.

Like walking in an English country garden, this cider has flowers everywhere; pot pourri, even the exotic Gewürztraminer grape come to mind. Light to medium in body, the palate is balanced with tropical fruits – think white melon, apricot and peach – with a long finish.

So how do the aromatics stand out with such clarity? Perhaps it's the unique temperature control during the second fermentation: water from a borehole 49m (160ft) deep comes up at a constant 11°C (51°F), bottles are loaded into crates and circulating water does the rest.

Quietly determined and philosophical, Franz doesn't want to have to produce cider on a schedule. The market can wait, he says. And, in a region dominated by wine, where the traditions of cider are all but lost, he wants 'to give our little farm a face'. For Magdalena, it's the love of crafting something of her own that appeals. Wineries just don't cut it.

'Cider must have its own character,' says Franz. 'The challenge is bringing the flavours through.' Floribunda more than meets the challenge.

floribunda
Apfel
Cider alla mela

Ramborn
CIDER CO.
Cellar Editions
ERBACHHOFER
SINGLE VARIETY
2016 HARVEST
Alc. 7,5% Vol 330ml
MEDIUM DRY STILL CIDER
from Luxembourg

RAMBORN
ERBACHHOFER, 2016

An apple called Rambo and a village called Born – that's the roots of Ramborn, Luxembourg's first cider producer.

Cider's history in this small country dates back thousands of years. Traditional, tall apple-tree orchards live alongside ancient perry pear trees and Ramborn, founded in 2014, is striving to revive, maintain and replant these heritage-rich orchards.

The story begins with three friends enjoying a cider during their travels in England. Today, founder Carlo Hein works with over 100 farmers, consulting with global experts including renowned educator Peter Mitchell and winemakers from France and Germany. Ramborn is also working with the local Biologische Station to help develop best practice guidelines for orchard management and maintenance.

Apple blends include varieties known elsewhere, like Boskoop and Bohnapfel, plus regional specialities such as Luxemburger Renette. Ramborn's range majors on blends but, when vintage conditions are really good, complex varieties like Erbachhofer get the solo treatment. Small and firm and renowned for its aromatics, Erbachhofer is regarded as the Sauer Valley's most distinctive apple.

Burnished gold in the glass, this is still and beautifully fragrant, with aromas of peach and apricot intertwined with a herbal hint. Medium dry, there's real breadth of fruit sweetness, with ripe yellow apple and tart kiwi fruit alongside zippy Granny Smith and tangerine zest, all accentuated with a delicate astringency redolent of starfruit.

And if you're wondering about whether there's a link with a certain movie franchise, yes, there is. To find out more, listen to CiderChat #129, recorded during CiderCon 2018, where podcast maestro Ria Windcaller chats with Carlo... it's well worth it.

region: Born, Luxembourg

fruit: the Erbachhofer apple, best known as one of the apples that goes into German *apfelwein*, or *viez* as it's called in Luxembourg

life story: harvested, fermented with white wine yeast for four weeks; one year ageing in stainless steel to round out the cider without compromising its vibrancy

abv: 7.5%

if you like this: try Perry, pears from ancient traditional orchards, including Bongert Altenhoven in Bettembourg; Original; Somerset Blend; Avalon

experience: visit Cider Haff (farm in Luxembourgish): shop, Wednesday–Sunday; tours, by reservation; orchard walks; follow social media for events news

ramborn.com

CIDRERIE DU VULCAIN
TROIS PÉPINS, 2013

region: Gruyère, Switzerland

fruit: equal parts apple, pear and quince, all foraged from unwanted, untreated trees

life story: natural yeast fermentation, with two or three light filtrations to ensure some residual sugar is left when bottled

abv: 5%

if you like this: try Poiré 2014 from 11 old pear varieties; Transparente 2015, four ancient varieties

experience: check out website for places in Europe and beyond to find Cidrerie du Vulcain; watch Facebook for events where Jacques will be

cidrelevulcain.ch

In the late 1990s, Jacques Perritaz had begun a new career. Leaving his post as a government biologist, he was off to be a winemaker. Only thing was, he became more fascinated with the wistful, forgotten old apple trees he passed on his travels. Next thing he knew, he was on the cider track. He found an old tile factory in Gruyère, converted it into a cidery and began making cider with endangered varieties.

That was in 2000 and his focus hasn't wavered since. Surrounded by the mountains, he works with dozens of rare apple varieties – and old pear varieties too. Some trees are up to 200 years old; all yield too little to be commercially viable. Looking like the Bruce Springsteen of the cider world, Jacques counts Eric Bordelet as his mentor, and also collaborates with pioneering pomologist Helmut Müller, himself the grower of over 300 apple varieties and 100 pear varieties.

Making a small, remarkably poised range of ciders, Jacques also draws upon quinces for perhaps his most well-known cider, Trois Pépins.

Named in honour of the three pome fruits that make up this blend – apple, pear and quince – this is incredibly fragrant. Very pale gold, with a fine sparkle, it's light to medium bodied, off-dry with a remarkably grown-up palate. There's a wonderful mix of the three pomes – quince adds a mellow yellowness to the whole affair, pear brings blossom and white flowers to the party while the apple provides the base structure and a balancing acidity. On the nose, there's almost an apple/custard pastry note. Who said cider couldn't be complex?

Cidrerie du Vulcain

Blak
St
QUINCY
JO & HOPS
EDITION
C

BLAKSTOC
QUINCY JO & HOPS EDITION

Over three-quarters of Austria's apples come from Styria, sitting as it does slap bang in the middle of what many call Europe's apple belt. And the region is also known for hops. So why not, Karl Karigl reasoned, see if the two might work together?

Why not indeed. And in Karl, they found the right researcher. Growing up in Styria, he had made cider since a teenager. Equipped with a degree in fermentation technology from Vienna University, this was a quest worth starting.

So, teaming up with three friends from Vienna, they came up with Blakstoc, using Styrian apples and hops from the Pacific Northwest in every cider, accentuating the individuality of each cider with a different set of extra ingredients.

The name Blakstoc means 'old tree' in high German, reflecting Blakstoc's love of heritage apple varieties and the art of foraging from wild trees. Over half of the mountainous regions of Styria are covered with forest.

So each of Karl's ciders includes Styrian hops. I've picked Quincy Jo. As well as a dash of quince, another pome fruit like apples and pears, the special ingredient here is blackcurrant – the Jo in the Quincy Jo being short for *johannisbeere*, German for blackcurrant. The hop notes appear on the finish, adding a welcome bitter flourish, while the blackcurrant notes roll around the palate.

This would be perfect as an aperitif, or with meat dishes accented by fruit, and with fruit desserts. Or instead of dessert. The balance here is key, with different elements hitting different parts of the palate at the same time. Medium in body and acidity, the fruit gives breadth; blackcurrants lend acidity and a touch more tannins to add to the apple tannins.

region: Styria, Austria

fruit: a blend of wild apples from the hills, Styrian blackcurrants

life story: fermentation takes place using beer yeast; the cider is dry hopped with Chinook and Centennial hops

abv: 4.5%

if you like this: try Ginger for my Honey; Wild Tree Hoppy; Buddha Hand Lemon

experience: follow social media for events where they are present

blakstoc.com

BRÄNNLAND
ISCIDER BARRIQUE, 2015

region: Västerbotten, Sweden

fruit: a blend of dessert apple varieties from Skåne and Västerbotten

life story: apples are pressed and the juice is frozen in December; cryoconcentration takes sugar levels to around 35 Brix; fermentation for 10–12 weeks, followed by one year in oak barriques, including some red wine barrels

abv: 11%

if you like this: try Iscider; Pernilla Perle, off-dry; Just Cider

experience: available in over a dozen countries, from Belgium and Denmark to the USA and UK, check website for details

www.brannlandcider.se

'The raw material decides what the end product is.' That's Andreas Sundgren of Brännland, 650km (400 miles) north of Stockholm on the Baltic Seaboard. While making his ice cider from the 2015 vintage, they tried to stop fermentation at 10% abv, but nature – the yeasts, the apples, the sugars – would not let him. So 11% is what it became.

While Brännland has other ciders in its range, Andreas made his name with his *isciders*. His original, fashioned from a special selection of dessert fruit, combines tangerines and tang on the palate, with refreshingly high acids in a showstopping fashion.

But it's the barrique-fermented *iscider* that makes these pages. It's exquisite. There's a herbal tinge to the marmalade-infused body. Cling peaches, apricots and *tarte tatin* notes abound alongside floral aromas. Slightly darker than the original, this retains that streak of acidity to balance, cleanse and refresh all at the same time. Although an inviting revelation right now, it will age and evolve.

Andreas makes his *iscider* according to the Québec PDO rules. That means that the original juice can only use 'natural' cold for cryoconcentration (see page 220), and the juice is frozen outside rather than in a cold store for the freeze–thaw process which concentrates the juice. 'You need a cold hit of -20 to -10°C (-4 to 14°F) for a few days,' he says.

Andreas is excited about his latest project: planting apple trees nearby at the Röbäcksdalen Field Station. 'They've never been planted that far north,' he says. 'We're going to plant Finnish and Russian apples, because they have the hardiness.'

'If cider is to become as respected as wine, it has to have ambition,' he says. Well, Andreas sure has that!

BRÄNNLAND
ISCIDER
FATLAGRAD
BARRIQUE
2015

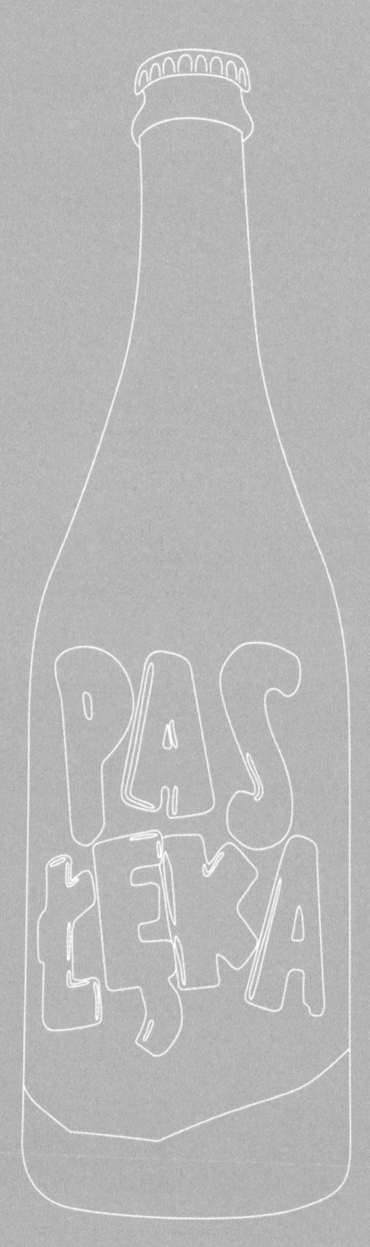
PAS
TEKA

KWAŚNE JABŁKO
PASŁĘKA, 2016

'We want to investigate which Polish varieties are good for cider,' says Marcin Wiechowski, co-founder of Kwaśne Jabłko. Marcin and wife Ewa exchanged the hustle and bustle of Warsaw for Masuria, the land of a thousand lakes, back in 2012. Since then, they have established Poland's first craft cidery.

Techniques initially learnt with Peter Mitchell in England have been honed with winemakers in Austria and wine importers in Poland. Now the pair have adopted the wild side. The orchards are organic and the fermentations primarily use native yeasts.

Working with dozens of varieties, international apples blend with indigenous ones. Favourites include the old Eastern European variety, Antonowka, with its floral aromas and fresh acidity, another old variety, Golden Reinette, with its complex spicy aromas, and Grafsztynek – the local name for American star, Gravenstein – with its uniquely delicate aromas and sometimes tropical flavours.

More orchards have been planted. 'Around 160 varieties, typical for north-east Europe,' says Marcin. But exploration doesn't stop there. 'We have also planted 250 trees of 20 British varieties,' he says, describing how much he appreciated working with England's Mid-Shires Orchard Group on this.

The ciders are named after local landmarks – our one here is named after the river Pasłęka. It's fragrant, light to medium bodied with a creamy sparkle. Aromas are peachy and autumnal, with very ripe apple notes blending into yellow fruit notes, wrapped up with a poised, balancing acidity.

But it doesn't stop with the orchards; the Wiechowskis have created an eco-haven, where visitors can be at one with nature while also understanding more about the unique possibilities afforded by the Polish expression of cider. Time for us all to do a little investigating.

region: Warmia, Poland

fruit: a blend of over 20 varieties, including local heroes, Grochówka, Glogierówka, and international stars, Grafsztynek (aka Gravenstein) and Jonathan

life story: apples are blended at pressing, natural fermentation in stainless steel; aged for at least three months before bottling

abv: 6.5%

if you like this: try Beczka nr 12; Wiosenny

experience: make a trip, book in at The Lodge; enjoy the tastings; enrol on workshops

kwasnejablko.pl

JAANIHANSO
BRUT, 2015

region: Pärnumaa, Estonia

fruit: a blend of locally grown apples, including several developed in Estonia in the 20th century and a few originating in Russia

life story: first fermentation using natural yeast; second fermentation over six months; light *dosage* at disgorging

abv: 8.5%

if you like this: try Rosé Méthode Traditionelle, with Estonian blackcurrants; Hopped Medium Cider, with Simcoe hops

experience: visit the cider house, confirm opening times beforehand; check Facebook for events

jaanihanso.ee

Back in the 13th century, apples were among the only fruits known in Estonia. Wild apple trees growing on the islands were joined in the 16th century by varieties from around the world. Finding a receptive climate, a culture of crafting cider at home – it's known as apple wine – sprang up. Yet, until the last few years, there were no commercial, orchard-focused cidermakers.

Enter Alvar and Veronika Roosimaa. Alvar made cider at home with his father when he was growing up. Working in the financial world, he longed to craft 'something physical'. So, inspired by the opportunities offered around his farm, an hour south of Talinn, he began exploring cider. A graduate of Peter Mitchell's course in the English countryside of Gloucestershire, Alvar also spent time at Burrow Hill in Somerset – 'Julian Temperley helped and inspired tremendously', he says.

Today, Jaanihanso has 5,500 trees, including some pears and sour cherries. While there are a few apples with mild tannins and characteristic spiciness, Alvar says the best ones for making cider are the late or very late ripening varieties. Here the sugars, acids and flavours have had most time to develop, with a classic example being Talvenauding. Developed in 1946 in Estonia with Swedish and German parentage, many consider it to be the Kingston Black of Estonia.

While it can go it alone, here it's part of the team in the Jaanihanso Brut. Very light golden in the glass, this is fragrant and floral throughout, with snappy bubbles, tangerine zest and pith on the palate, light starfruit-like astringency from the tannins, and lemon citrus on the finish.

'We are very much *terroir*-focused cidermakers,' says Alvar. That's for sure.

BRUT

USA & CANADA

Apple trees arrived in **America** with the settlers. Producing handy balls of sweetness and energy, presidents installed orchards, and it became a regulation for anyone setting up in Ohio to plant at least 50 trees.

The legends surrounding folk hero Johnny Appleseed may be a little sanitised – as Michael Pollan points out in *The Botany of Desire*, the wildlings that sprout from an ungrafted pip are too bitter to eat. Johnny's popularity in the early 19th century, he says, was probably more due to him giving his customers fruit with which to make cider.

By then, some of America's original heritage varieties had already become established. Gravenstein, dating back to Europe in the 1600s, was doing well, as was Newtown Pippin, a New York-born variety from 1720. Northern Spy, another New York creation, arrived around 1800.

And that's what characterises much of the American cider scene – the apples and pears are different. Different flavour profiles and, crucially, different levels of tannins. Couple this with the creativity and ingenuity always on offer in America, and it's not surprising that there's such a sense of excitement.

There are over 800 commercial cideries in 48 of the USA's 50 states, with the top three – New York, Michigan and California – responsible for a third of that number.

America is following a twin-track approach with its ciders. On the one hand, *terroiristes* hold fast to a strong alliance between orchard and cider, whether

EXPLORE

Cidre de Québec: cidreduquebec.com

New York State Cider Association: newyorkcider association.com

Northwest Cider Association: nwcider.com

United States Association of Cider Makers: ciderassociation.org

Cider Guide: US & Canada Cider Festivals: ciderguide. com/cider-festivals

British Columbia Cider Week, April/ May: bcciderweek. com

Cider Weeks, New York State: ciderweeknewyork. com

Franklin County Cider Days, November: ciderdays.org

Gravenstein Apple Fair, August: gravensteinapple fair.com

Le Mondial des Cidres, Montreal, March: mondial descidres.com

Along Came a Cider, Meredith Collin: alongcameacider. blogspot.com

CiderCraft: cidercraftmag.com

Cider Chat, Ria Windcaller, the world's leading cider podcaster: ciderchat. com

Cider•Culture: ciderculture.com

Cider/Food, Ryan Burk & Eva Deitch: ciderfood.com

this is via heritage blends or ciders crafted with tannin-rich varieties, as pioneered by Steve Wood at Poverty Lane Orchards/Farnum Hill. This also includes the growing trend towards foraging. On the other hand, new-wave cidermakers, such as Reverend Nat's Hard Cider, are widening the recipes to craft any number of novel flavours.

What has characterised the US cider scene in recent years has been its spirit of openness. The United States Association of Cider Makers offers an invigorating annual CiderCon gathering, while cidermaker associations in the Northwest, New York, Michigan and Pennsylvania are similarly welcoming.

Cornell University continues with its impressive research programme and trial nurseries to explore how to enable orchards – and cidermakers – to give of their best. And consumer events such as Franklin County Cider Days serve to share the worlds of orchards and ciders with a growing audience.

Meanwhile **Canada**, where cider production wasn't made legal until the 1970s, is playing catch-up. Apple growing is focused on the east and west coast regions, and the same feeling of freedom pervades the scene as due south in the USA. One specialty is ice cider, which secured its own protected designation of origin in 2014. Christian Barthomeuf, now behind Clos Saragnat, is a pioneer of this delectable style.

Today, the American revolution has reached the digital world – see Explore sidebar – and the cider tap. Places like Schilling Cider House in Portland, The Northman in Chicago, Stem's Acreage restaurant in Lafayette, Colorado, Angry Orchard's Innovation Cider House, Walden, NY, and, of course, Anxo in Washington DC, are beacons of great cider and perry. You'll find many of these in this chapter. And those that aren't – next time!

DRAGON'S HEAD
TRADITIONAL CIDER

region: Vashon Island, Washington State, USA

fruit: traditional English and French cider apples

life story: late picking, natural yeasts, long fermentation; a year in tank prior to bottling, to allow the tannins to harmonise; 'there's a lot of bittersweet fruit in there'

abv: 7.4%

if you like this: try Manchurian Cider, based around crab apples; single-varietal Pippin

experience: hop on the ferry from Seattle, visit the tasting room, open Friday–Sunday all year; Vashon Cider Festival; follow Instagram for event news

dragonsheadcider.com

'We found the ciders that we enjoyed were made with those sorts of apples,' says Laura Cherry, speaking about cider varieties, as she explained how she and husband Wes created waves in 2010. Despite Washington being the top apple-producing state in the USA, at the time it had no cider fruit to speak of.

The Cherrys changed that. They found Vashon Island in the Puget Sound across the bay from Seattle. Not only a beautiful spot, but its maritime climate far more suited to these apples.

They gathered varieties. Last count they had around 75, with 25 leading the charge. French apples like Reine des Pommes and Muscat de Dieppe share orchard space with English classics like Dabinett and Kingston Black. Harrison, one of America's only true cider varieties, also features. 'There's lots of onesies and twosies,' says Wes.

And what's in the blend for their Traditional Cider? 'There's Dabinett,' says Wes. 'I adore that tree – it's got apricot and peach notes. Stoke Red, Chisel Jersey... oh, and Vilberie too...' He could go on!

The sheer multiplicity comes through on the palate, as does their insistence on full-flavoured apples from the get-go. The fruit is left to ripen on the tree as long as possible, and even when it's harvested, many weeks can go by before pressing. This shows in fine bittersweet notes and a tangible, elegant texture, flavours of apple snow surrounded by notes of apple-and-peach crumble.

At the moment, around two-thirds of their ciders are fermented with natural yeasts. That proportion is likely to grow. 'We just think it's far more layered,' says Laura. Once more, the apple leads the way.

DRAGON'S HEAD
TRADITIONAL CIDER
ESTATE BITTERSWEET APPLES

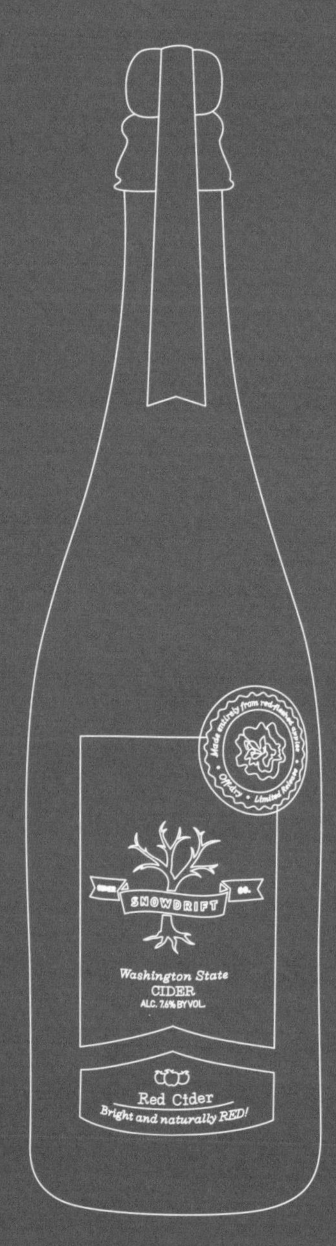
Made entirely from red-fleshed apples
Off-dry • Limited Release
SNOWDRIFT
CO.
Washington State
CIDER
ALC. 7.6% BY VOL.
Red Cider
Bright and naturally RED!

SNOWDRIFT
RED CIDER

'Until about 10–15 years ago I didn't like apples at all. I thought they were either too sweet or tasted like a potato, depending on the time of year. Cider apples – red-fleshed apples, sports and seedlings – have changed me from firmly apple agnostic to fanatic!'

Tim Larsen, cidermaker at family cider producer Snowdrift, is talking about what goes into their rather special Red Cider. Not just called Red, but naturally red. No berry additions whatsoever.

One weekend when he was doing the local farmers' market a few years ago, the farmer selling these apples – they originated in Switzerland – offered him a 'small sample'. Next thing 40 bins of apples arrived. 'They overwhelmed our tiny facility!'

'I've absolutely fallen in love with these apples and Red has become our most popular product,' Tim says.

There are eight varieties, all descendents from Kazakhstan's wild apple forests, and, as you'd expect, they each behave differently. When fermented separately, each identifies with a specific fruit, says Tim. For example, watermelon, cranberry and strawberry. Like secret agents, they have numbers as names. Tim particularly likes 26-05. 'It carries most of the colour – usually...' he says. 'It also tends to be very punchy when it comes to acidity and has a bright cherry characteristic.'

But what's it like in the glass? Sure enough, there are aromas of cherries and almonds on the nose, with light, fresh acid upfront, a fleshy stone fruit on the mid-palate. Medium dry, this is superbly integrated with a soft, fuzzy astringency.

Tim is still in touch with the orchardist. This year he's been offered some new varieties. Expect some more liquid history...

region: Wenatchee Valley, Washington, USA

fruit: a blend of eight red-fleshed apples, collectively known as the Redwave

life story: harvested over four to six weeks; pressed when fully ripe; fermentation; at least three months' ageing; light carbonation

abv: 7.5%

if you like this: try Orchard Select, with its bittersharp component; Perry Reserve, *méthode champenoise*, with Washington-grown, true perry pears

experience: Tasting Room; farmers' markets; check social media for news of festivals; Cider Club

snowdriftcider.com

LIBERTY CIDERWORKS
PORTER'S PERFECTION 2016

region: Spokane, Washington State, USA

fruit: bittersweet Porter's Perfection from Bishops' Orchards and Steury Orchards

life story: for small batches, rack and cloth press; wild yeast; three months of fermentation plus further four months resting in barrel before bottling

abv: 8.6%

if you like this: try Manchurian Crabapple, an intense flavour experience; Stonewall Barrel Aged

experience: visit the Tap Room, Thursday–Sunday; join the Core Club (someone had to do that!); follow social media for events news; Seattle Cider Summit, September; Vashon Ciderfest, October

libertycider.com

Now that's what I call a 'small batch'. Just 12 cases! Via the good hands of several kind cider folk – take a bow Rick, Darlene, Dan, Edu and Martin (that's another story for another time) – we had ourselves a rare treat.

It's real pumpkin orange in the glass. On the nose, there's notes of tangerine, warm oranges and yellow apple, plus a whiff of the barrel. The palate shows more of the same fruit, with lovely Seville orange rind, ripe autumnal fruit. It's still, with fine, delicate tannins of great persistence.

Based in Spokane, eastern Washington, Rick Hastings and Austin Dickey set up Liberty Ciderworks in 2013, having both been hobby cidermakers for a while. They are inspired by classic heirloom varieties such as Winesap and Gravenstein, and the English cider traditions. As if to prove a point, their English Style won Gold in GLINTCAP the year after they began.

Fruit is sourced mainly from two renowned farms, both of which specialise in heirloom and English and French varieties. Bishops' Orchards is bang in the middle of Palouse, previously only prized for wheat – until now – while Steury Orchards is just over the border in Idaho.

Porter's Perfection originated over in Somerset, and was developed by – you guessed it – a Mr Porter, Charles in this case. It is a small, dark red bittersharp apple that arrives relatively late. Normally, it's purely a good team player in the blend, but Rich was thrilled when he came across it. 'I loved the flavour profile,' he says. Now it's going to be a regular.

Cider is a form of art, say Rick and Austin on their website. Bold words indeed. But in Rick and Austin's case it's true.

LIBERTY
CIDERWORKS
RESERVE SERIES CIDER
PORTER'S PERFECTION
SINGLE-VARIETAL
INLAND NW GROWN • 750ML

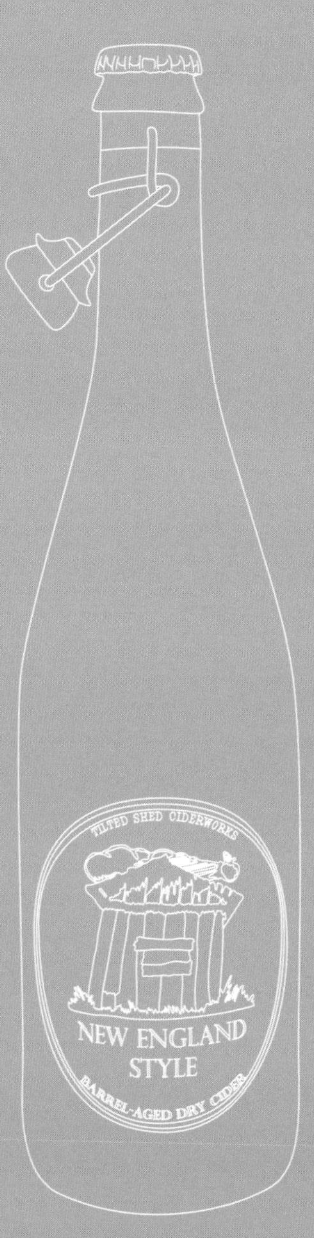
TILTED SHED CIDERWORKS
NEW ENGLAND
STYLE
BARREL-AGED DRY CIDER

TILTED SHED CIDERWORKS
NEW ENGLAND STYLE

With 100 varieties of cider apples and perry pears in the ground, plus their own pomological research game plan, it's a given that Scott Heath and Ellen Cavalli's ciders at Tilted Shed are going to prove fascinating. I'd tasted a couple at CiderCon 2018, when eloquent cider aficionadoes Darlene Hayes and Dan Pucci explored the *terroir* consequences of Newtown Pippin in the US. Darlene graciously helped me try a couple more, including the New England Style, which, cuckoo-like, edged out original contender Graviva for the Tilted Shed spot in the book.

A complex treat, this is inspired by the recipes from the early settlers' time rather than a direct copy. One way to stop cider from going bad back then was to add some form of sugar, often maple syrup, plus raisins to kick off a second fermentation, thus raising the alcohol and protecting the cider.

Here, yes, the alcohol is raised to 10%, but it's the barrel influence and resulting complexity that fascinates. While the sparkle isn't a streamer – in my glass at least – there's a gentle prickle on the tongue. Golden yellow in colour, funky notes from the barrel hit you first – warm lemons, marshmallow, cloves, star anise, mint, even. On the medium-bodied palate, these flavours are mellowed with warm orange, sweet thick-cut marmalade and ripe peach notes, rounded off with fine tannins.

Back to Scott and Ellen for the final word: 'Our mission is to elevate the apple to greatness by making world-class ciders that are revelatory and sublime, with a distinct sense of place and point of view.' Mission accomplished, I'd say.

region: Sonoma County, California, USA

fruit: organic, dry-farmed Rhode Island Greenings, Jonathans, from Vulture Hill Orchard, Sebastopol

life story: molasses and raisins added when first fermentation almost finished, allowed to referment, before bottling with brown sugar for bottle conditioning

abv: 10%

if you like this: try Graviva, a 50:50 blend with heirloom/French bittersweets; join Cider Club waiting list

experience: visit Tasting Room, Saturday; subscribe to *Malus* ciderzine; watch website Events tab for cidermaking and cider pairing workshop news; tune into Sonoma County Farm Trails; Gravenstein Apple Fair, August

tiltedshed.com

STEM CIDERS
COLORADO HERITAGE BLEND

region: Denver, Colorado, USA

fruit: a blend of the classic English varietal Dabinett with the even older, aromatic American heirloom, Winesap, from Colorado Western Slope

life story: cool fermentation with a neutral wine yeast to preserve aromatic, no malolactic fermentation; bottled two weeks later

abv: 7.2%

if you like this: try L'Acier, a fragrant Michigan blend; Coffee Apple Cider, a toasty collaboration with Method Roasters

experience: visit RiNo Taproom, Denver Arts District; Acreage Ciderhouse, Lafayette; join in Firkin Monday each month, to share the new small-batch ciders; CiderGrass festival, Acreage

stemciders.com; acreageco.com

In Michigan, cider and doughnuts are an autumn tradition. For the young, it will be apple juice and doughnuts. That's how it started with Eric Foster, co-founder of Stem Cider in Colorado. 'It's just a part of who you are,' he tells me. He graduated to working in his local cider mill where he learned the ropes during his teenage years, before following his outdoor tendencies and moving to the Centennial State for university.

Fast forward a decade or so, and during a cidery visit back home with friend and fellow Michigander, Phil Kao, the two hatch a plan. Why not set up a cidery in Colorado? Phil, an engineer by training and an avid chef, was keen.

A few years later, in 2013, Stem opened for business. Named in honour of plants themselves rather than a location, Stem draws on fruit from a number of states – Washington, Michigan, Colorado to name but three. This arrives as juice, milled and pressed to their spec.

I'm tasting the most local, the Colorado Heritage Blend. It's incredibly fragrant, with aromas of apple and orange blossom, wallflowers even. The palate is light to medium in weight, with lemon citrus notes on the finish, barely discernible tannins, and well-judged crispness. With its balanced acids this will be good with food. Perhaps a young goat's cheese or Manchego; white fish or meat; even a Greek salad.

The guys have just opened their second restaurant, Acreage, in nearby Lafayette. With views across the hill, an 5-ha (12-acre) orchard and two of the hottest chefs consulting on the Basque-inspired menu, Eric and Phil look set to be creating their own, highly sociable cider tradition. Wassail.

COLORADO
HERITAGE
BLEND
GLUTEN FREE
STEM
CIDER
DNVR · COLO

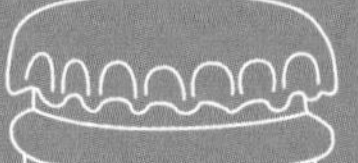
PREMIUM
Uncle John's
HARD CIDER
MELDED

UNCLE JOHN'S CIDER MILL
MELDED

'No one eats more apples in September and October than Mike Beck!' The gregarious Mike is explaining to me that this is the best way to assess the state of sugars, starches and acids prior to harvest.

And harvest-time at Uncle John's is frantic. Not only are there hundreds of tonnes of apples and pears heading to the mill – you can go and watch if you pick the right day – over 300,000 visitors flock to the Cider Mill for the annual autumn ritual of 'cider' (the soft version, freshly pressed juice to you and me) and doughnuts.

It was Mike's parents, John and Carolyn, who diversified the fruit business into a family-friendly destination in the 1970s. Mike went one step further, spotting the potential for 'hard' cider, beginning the cider business in 2003 with his wife Dede.

So difficult choosing which of Mike's ciders to feature. Like the man himself, one of the founding fathers of the US Association of Cider Makers, the ciders are generous of spirit and full of character. His Old Standard cider, for example, blends fruit from trees at least 50 years old. He doesn't want to lose these heirlooms. 'I've just "found" another 5ha (12 acres),' he tells me excitedly. 'It's all about soul.'

But it's the Melded that captures my heart. Marrying English and French cider apples with American heirlooms, it's a meeting of nations. 'It's a term my grandmother used to use when playing Canasta,' explains Mike. 'You meld your deck.'

With Uncle John's Melded, we have the broad, sweet-fruited palate from three-quarters bittersweet and bittersharp apples melded with the generous brightness from the sharp apples. Truly multicultural.

region: St John's, Michigan, USA

fruit: bittersweets from England and France, including Dabinett, Kingston Black, Calville Blanc, Pomme Gris, blended with American sharps and bittersharps, including Baldwin, Harrison, Wickson

life story: apples fermented together, cellared in tank for nine months, with proportion in barrel; blending and bottling

abv: 6.5%

if you like this: try Old Standard and Perry; ask about the specials when you visit

experience: Tasting Room, Uncle John's Cider Mill: March–May, weekends; June–December, all week; Fall Season, Cider Mill; check dates to buy juice to make your own cider

ujcidermill.com

TANDEM CIDERS
FARMHOUSE

region: Leelanau Peninsula, Michigan, USA

fruit: classic American heirloom varieties, Northern Spy, Jonagold, Rhode Island Greening

life story: blends, 2014 and 2015; the heirloom blend spent seven months in American oak barrels; blended and bottled spring 2016

abv: 5.6%

if you like this: try elegant Green Man; sassy The Crabster

experience: visit Tasting Room, check winter and summer hours, Mid-Mitten Cider Festival, Uncle John's Cider Mill

tandemciders.com

Back in the early noughties, a couple arrived at Heathrow Airport in London from America, complete with tandem. Cycling out of the airport, I doubt whether those they were to meet would realise how pivotal this month-long break was going to be.

Both beer lovers – they had met in the brewpub that he was running – pubs were inevitably on the itinerary. And when the beer failed to sparkle, there was cider. And what cider! Not like anything they'd tasted before.

Five years later Dan Young and Nikki Rothwell established Tandem Ciders in Leelanau Peninsula, known as Michigan's pinkie because of its location and shape, bang in the middle of wine country. Fast-forward 10 years, and the mix of Dan's brewing knowledge and Nikki's agricultural background has proved the perfect blend. Richard Burton heads up cidermaking, cider trees have been planted, and there's a sense of purpose and fun in the cidery.

Most of the ciders are punchy blends, with trademark clarity and direction. Farmhouse is no exception. A sassy mix from two different vintages, it's bright and tart, the floral nature of the aromas is enchanting, and the clean, lengthy finish is memorable and enjoyable.

Blend number one, the historic heirlooms, spent seven months in American oak barrels. Blend number two is a true mixed bag, Richard tells me, coming from a 70-year-old orchard at nearby John Kilcherman's renowned Christmas Cove Farm. The mix includes plenty of russeted varieties, plus others like Sheep's Nose, Yarlington Mill, and the wonderfully named Winter Banana.

The words that encircle the logo on the label are fun too. This one says 'Fit for a Brit'. Certainly is.

LIFE IS SWEET LIFE IS HARD
FARMHOUSE
TANDEM
CIDERS
FIT FOR A BRIT
5.6%
ALC BY VOL
750ML
(25.4 FL OZ)
HARD APPLE CIDER
HANDCRAFTED

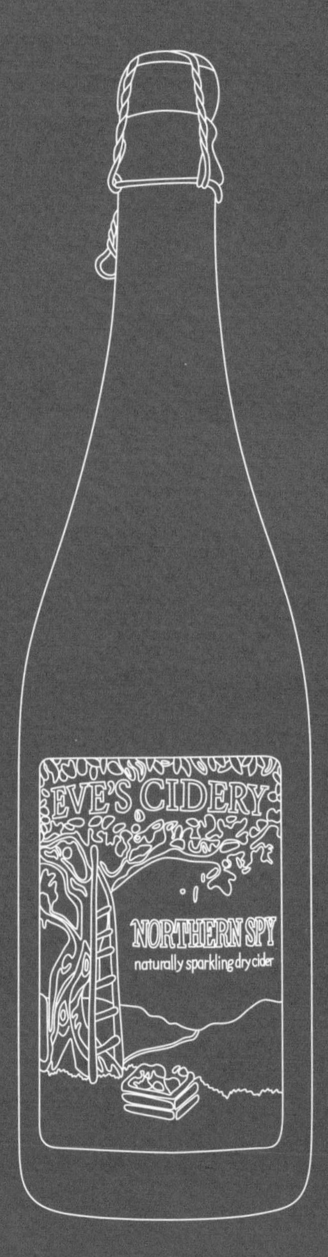
EVE'S CIDERY
NORTHERN SPY
naturally sparkling dry cider

EVE'S CIDERY
NORTHERN SPY, 2016

Within days of seeing Steve Wood on the cover of *Fruit Growers News* back in 1999, Autumn Stoscheck drove eight hours across New England to find him at his orchards in New Hampshire. She was working as an apprentice at an orchard. Not yet 20, she was in love with the rhythm of pruning. He was the pioneer growing cider fruit in the USA. Here were apple varieties specific to cider. Autumn was transfixed.

Recognising a determined talent, Steve not only shared his scion wood with her, he took her through his cellar, with tastings of the various barrels, pointing out sharps, bittersharps and bittersweets. And thus it began. A year or so later in 2001, Autumn plunged her waitressing savings into Eve's Cidery, partnering with sixth-generation orchardist James Cummins, a link that continues to this day.

Now husband Ezra Sherman shares the duties. Autumn draws on fruit from several orchards, including her grandmother's, which they have replanted. They are organic, and she waits for the apples to fall, believing that the quality of fruit is 'radically improved' this way.

Modest and creative, it's inspiring walking with Autumn on a crisp, snow-strewn day through her hillside orchards. There's a fascinating intensity in her approach, which follows through in her ciders.

This Northern Spy came from one of James's orchards. Light gold with a vibrant stream of tiny bubbles, you can imagine those trees nestling in the hills. Aromatic, the fruit sweetness reminds you of Russet apples, Cox's Orange Pippins and zesty tangerines. Dry with beautiful autumnal notes, as it warms it becomes more rounded, with flavours that evolve into tart peach and orchard fruit salad.

2016 was a challenging vintage all round. Autumn's trees responded with more complexity, more depth. You can tell she's proud of them.

region: Finger Lakes, New York, USA

fruit: Northern Spy, one of New England's favourite heirlooms, prized for its tart sweetness; allegedly named after a legendary 19th-century abolitionist

life story: first fermentation in tank, second in bottle; only 50 cases produced

abv: 9.2%

if you like this: try Albee Hill 2016, dry, still; Darling Creek 2016, off-dry, sparkling

experience: book a cider tasting online, July–September; Ithaca farmers' market, weekends; check Facebook

evescidery.com

BLACK DIAMOND CIDER
SLATESTONE

region: Finger Lakes, New York, USA

fruit: blend of English cider varieties, including Porter's Perfection, Dabinett and Brown Snout, with classic heirlooms, such as Newtown Pippin, Gold Rush and Golden Russet

life story: named with reference to underlying geology; a cool fermentation, initially wild then cultured yeast; light carbonation

abv: 8.3%

if you like this: try RabbleRouser, blend of American heirloom, English bittersweets, and red-fleshed rarities; Hickster, blend of Russet and bittersweets

experience: Finger Lakes Cider Week, group tours: history of cider, apples and orchards; Ithaca farmers' market, July–December, weekends, check social media, join mailing list

blackdiamondcider.com; incredapple.com

'What started as a bad situation was really serendipitous because New York State got a head start on growing high tannin varieties.' Ian Merwin, emeritus horticulture professor at Cornell University, is describing how Cornell landed up with hundreds of bittersweet and bittersharp trees thanks to the sale of Bulmers to Scottish & Newcastle in 2003. Ian's team had been nurturing 10,000 cider trees which the cidermaking giant had invested in but then had to abandon. Cornell's orchard became that bit larger.

Ian had returned to New York from California nearly 20 years earlier with his wife Jackie. While the day job focused on plant science and pomology, the cider journey began while they were house-sitting. 'There was lots of good, abandoned orchard fruit,' explains Ian. 'We took care of their trees and used all of their apples for our first batch of cider,' says Jackie.

While the pair established Black Diamond Farm, specialising in heirloom varieties, Ian became one of the godfathers of the modern cider movement, dispensing global wisdom and practical advice in equal measure.

Now the Merwins have three orchards. Benefitting from the mellowing influence of the nearby Finger Lakes, they grow 145 different varieties, over 35 of which go into Slatestone, the sprightly, golden cider in my glass.

Pale gold in colour, Slatestone is beautifully dry, with apricot, peach and lemon aromas alongside wallflowers and warm, sun-baked stone. A light sparkle that lingers alongside tangerine and grapefruit on the palate leads to a long finish.

A number of Spanish cider trees were being planted when we last spoke. 'They're finally coming out of quarantine,' says Ian. 'I brought those in 2002.' A patient visionary.

BLACK
DIAMOND
CIDER
SLATESTONE

POMME
SUR LIE
STILL AND DRY
SOUTH HILL CIDER
ITHACA NEW YORK

SOUTH HILL CIDER
POMME SUR LIE, 2015

'I think the next generation of cider orchards will be trees like these because they're more disease resistant.' Steve Selin, South Hill Cider, is sharing the patch of wild trees he and a band of fellow cidermakers forage from in the autumn. 'A lot of the English and French varieties, they flower so early and are prone to fireblight,' he continues. 'Even if you're organic, you have to spray something for fireblight. But if you can get native trees like this that flower at a good time and taste great, then these could be the future cider orchards around here.'

Steve is renowned for his ability to blend feral apples with those from other orchards. Never happier than when out pruning, his own orchard is planted with 1,500 trees, one row per variety, except for a few favourites, like Porter's Perfection, which gets double billing, and Dabinett, with four rows to its name.

Several of his ciders, like Pomme Sur Lie, major on the wild side. Barrel fermented and aged, the warmed apricot scents mix with a herbal tinge. It's gleaming gold in the glass, still and dry, with a breadth of beautiful stone fruit, heading into cling peach and apricots, plus lemon zest and hints of vanilla. Medium bodied, the tannins are remarkably integrated and the acidity balances the purity of the fruit.

An acclaimed fiddle player, Steve is also a long-time supporter of the Finger Lakes Apple Tree Project, designed to rescue, record and reclaim unwanted trees and forgotten orchards. There's a visionary here as well as an archivist.

region: Finger Lakes, New York, USA

fruit: foraged apples from Finger Lakes National Park; the progeny of heirloom varieties brought over from Europe

life story: fermented in barrel with natural yeasts; aged nine months on the lees in four-to six-year-old French barrels

abv: 8.2%

if you like this: try PackBasket, 100% foraged; Stone Fence Farm, single orchard cider with over 20 French and English cider varieties

experience: follow happenings on social media; check events on Facebook; Cider Club

southhillcider.com

BLACKDUCK CIDERY
PERRY, 2016

region: Finger Lakes, New York, USA

fruit: six pears, Huffcap, the heirloom Seckel, plus wild pears, including the 'cheese-pear'

life story: slow fermentation with wild yeasts; unfiltered, unfined; bottle conditioned

abv: 6.7%

if you like this: try Percy Percy, based on English cider varieties; Crabby Pip, with a third crab apples; Woody, fermented and aged in Hungarian oak

experience: Tasting Room, weekends; pruning workshops, spring; check Daringdrake.com for Ithaca farmers' market and Blackduck Cidery Farmstand news

blackduckcidery.com

'Now my big thing is we are grafting a lot of wild pears that we have found that have perry qualities. Tannins or high acid. These are from groves in the National Forest, anywhere from 40 to 100 years old, with no fireblight.' John Diamond at Blackduck Cidery, is explaining how he and fellow founder, Shannon, have got round the devastating situation caused by fireblight a few years ago.

Turns out perry pears are particularly susceptible to this voracious bacterium. 'I'd never seen anything like it,' he says. 'It was travelling about a metre (two to three feet) in a day.' Being organic made it harder, but with resilience they got it under control. And now their perry repertoire is all the richer, with the addition of wild-grafted pears from the forest.

'This one has the "cheese-pear" in,' he says of the 2016 perry in our glasses. 'That's my favourite. That's the wild one. It smells like cheese when you pick it.' (Luckily the smell disappears by the time milling happens a few weeks later!)

This is exquisite. There's a tantalising bouquet, a mix of blossom, green apple, pineapple and Cox's Orange Pippin. The palate is textured, with pear and orange notes, and a long finish. As with all Blackduck ciders and perries, there's a generous, natural complexity, no doubt due in part to John's non-interventionist principles.

Known equally for their free-spirited ciders, John and Shannon grow hundreds of apple and pear varieties. The next generation, Idunn and Pippin, are often in the orchards too. The legacy is in safe hands.

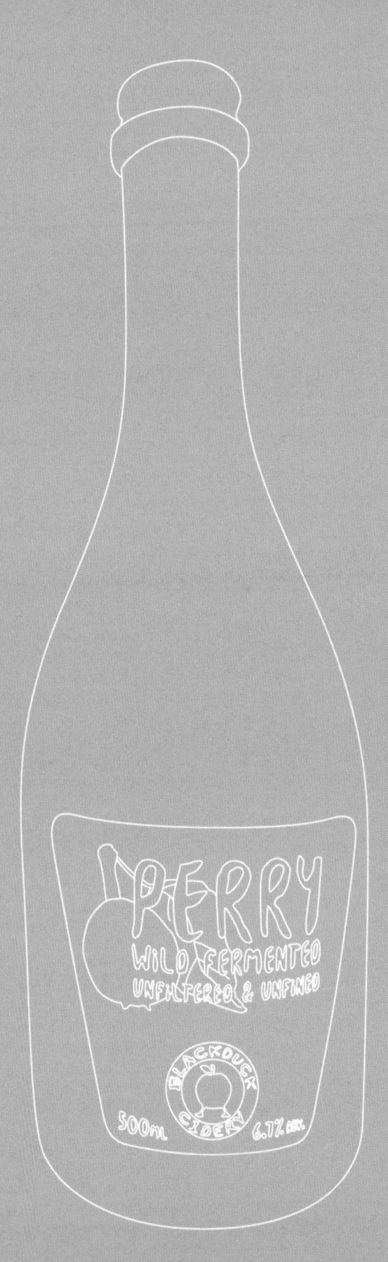
PERRY
WILD FERMENTED
UNFILTERED & UNFINED
BLACKDUCK
CIDER
500ml
6.7% ABV.

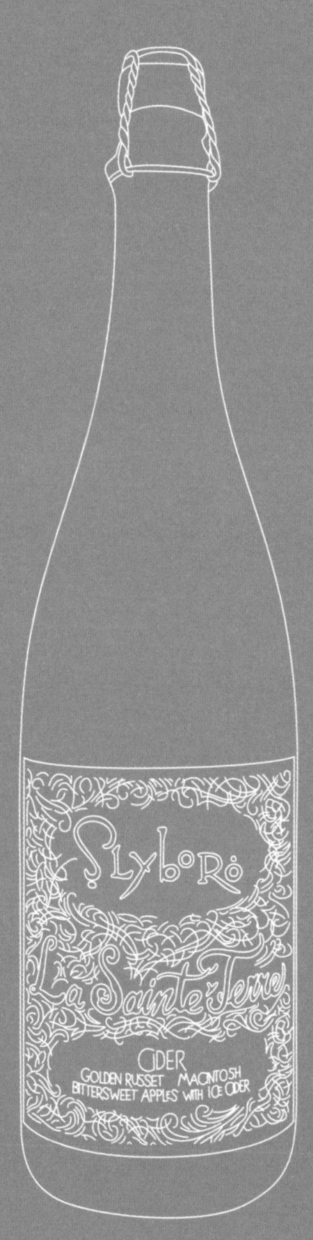
Slyboro
La Sainte Terre
CIDER
GOLDEN RUSSET MACINTOSH
BITTERSWEET APPLES WITH ICE CIDER

SLYBORO
LA SAINTE TERRE

Pick-your-own is a huge tradition in the foothills of the Adirondacks. Nowhere is this more popular than Hicks Orchard, with generations coming to enjoy cider doughnuts as they gather up apples and blueberries. There's been another side to the story for the last decade or so.

'I knew from history that everyone used to make cider. It was deeply threaded through our culture,' Dan Wilson tells me of the beginnings of Slyboro. Determined to revive the art and tradition, he and his then wife, Susan, set about learning from those whose grandfathers used to have a 'barrel in the basement'. Working with Cornell oenology department, they crafted distinctive ciders, still and sparkling. And ice ciders too.

La Sainte Terre straddles two of these camps, with nearly a fifth of the blend being ice cider. The main blend marries bittersweet varieties with regional apples, including the florally scented McIntosh, and Dan's favourite, Golden Russet, with its rich aromas and baking spice note.

The result? It's fascinating. A sassy balance of sweetness, acidity and sparkle, with a light herbaceous streak. We're in melon cocktail territory here with wonderful aromatics. Cooked, warm peach and apricot, yellow fruits – pineapple, yellow apples – and exotic perfumed flowers. The palate is sumptuous and rounded.

And what of the name? Dan has been inspired by a number of writings by famed American essayist Henry David Thoreau. In one, he describes the roots of the word 'saunter', as *la sainte terre*, 'the sacred earth, almost as a pilgrimage'. Elsewhere Thoreau speaks of 'the culmination of his saunter [was] to find this particular wild apple tree', says Dan. It's all about 'the idea of connecting with nature in a deep way'.

region: Hudson Valley, New York, USA

fruit: Golden Russet, McIntosh plus bittersweet apples like Yarlington Mill, Chisel Jersey and Dabinett; ice cider, a culinary blend, including McIntosh, Jonagold, Northern Spy

life story: varieties fermented separately; ice cider produced using cryoconcentration, natural freeze-thaw cycles

abv: 8.5%

if you like this: try still Kingston Black; Hidden Star; Ice Harvest

experience: farmers' markets; Tasting Room, July onwards – check hours; Paint & Cider; check Facebook for further events

slyboro.com

HUDSON VALLEY FARMHOUSE CIDER
NORTHERN SPY CIDER, 2016

region: Hudson Valley, New York, USA

fruit: Northern Spy

life story: unfiltered, bottle conditioned

abv: 6.3%

if you like this: try God Speed the Plough, blend of Dabinett with heirloom Hudson Valley apples; buy a Farmhouse Hard Cider Kit

experience: Stone Ridge Orchard Tasting Room, May–October; Union Square Green Market; Hudson Valley Cider Week; Cider Week New York

hudsonvalleyfarmhousecider.com;

stoneridgeorchard.us/fruitstand

Northern Spy is a venerable, historic apple and one of America's classic heirlooms. Discovered in the early 19th century in north-western New York, while there's some debate about the origins of its name, there's no question about its popularity, particularly in the New England states.

'It's very biennial but has a wonderful flavour and texture,' says Elizabeth Ryan, founder and cidermaker at Hudson Valley Farmhouse Cider. While its bright acidity is assured, 'it needs to hang for its full aromatics to develop,' she says, adding that 2016 saw her apples 'fighting for that extra sugar'.

An orchardist of some repute, Elizabeth learnt her cidermaking art in Somerset and Herefordshire as well as at Cornell University. 'It is the alchemy of the whole process,' she says when asked what inspires her. She grows over 100 varieties of apple, including several in her young cider fruit orchard. The Northern Spy Cider is fashioned at her Breezy Hill Orchard.

Pure gold in colour, this is beautifully clear with a delicate sparkle. Floral aromas mixed with baked apple. There's a delightful texture on the medium-bodied palate, with flavours of fresh peach and very ripe apple throughout. The orchard fruits continue to the close, with good, balancing crispness and a long finish. Enjoy solo or partner with white meat or fish, orange- or peach-infused salad.

Elizabeth recounts with obvious happiness being persuaded at the outset to visit Sheppy's in Somerset for its Wassail ceremony as a guest of Richard Sheppy. 'I went and it changed my life,' she says. 'We've been wassailing our orchard ever since.' Seems to be working then.

HUDSON VALLEY
FARMHOUSE CIDER

SPY CIDER

Unfiltered & Bottle Conditioned

ABV 6.3%

Valley Flor
ANGRY
ORCHARD
HARD CIDER
750ml

ANGRY ORCHARD
FIRST FLORA, 2015

'It's all about the UK. It's where it all began.' So says the modest Ryan Burk, master cidermaker in charge of all Angry Orchard's ciders – and now perries. We're catching a word after he's waltzed off with the top international trophy at the historic Royal Bath & West Championship in 2017 for First Flora 2015, the first of his small batch series. He also snaffled silverware for a number of his other ciders.

Ryan is talking about his time with Herefordshire cider wizard, Tom Oliver. 'Tom has been my gateway,' he says. Certainly, since they met when Ryan was at Virtue Cider – his entry into the professional cider world – the respect has been mutual. Several fascinating collaborations have ensued and they've both been racking up the air miles.

But First Flora is all Ryan's. With Angry Orchard since 2015, this is his first cider from the fledgling trees planted at Angry Orchard's Innovation Orchard in the apple belt of New York State. And it's a stupendous start. Golden in colour, aromas of baked apple, spice and ginger on the nose flow seamlessly onto a complex palate, where soft, sour acidity is neatly balanced with a nice bitterness. Fermented using natural yeasts, this has spent time maturing in Calvados barrels before release. Full bodied, it is pleasingly dry with lovely fruit.

'I want to make cider in America not a fad, but a noble beverage,' he says. 'The most exciting hasn't happened yet.' What you have in your glass is the beginning.

region: Walden, New York State, USA

fruit: a blend of bittersweet and sharp apples

life story: natural yeasts, aged for several months in Calvados barrels

abv: 6%

if you like this: check out Understood in Motion series, including 02, the collaboration with EZ Orchards, and 03, the collaboration with Tom Oliver (see page 10); Asturian-style Edu

experience: head to Innovation Cider House in Walden, NY, for the tours, including Barrel Room or Treehouse Tours (spring–autumn), taproom, exhibition, cider garden (weekends)

angryorchard.com/our-orchard

EDEN SPECIALTY CELLARS
VERMONT ICE CIDER, HEIRLOOM BLEND

region: Newport, Vermont, USA

fruit: a blend of 15 apples, including Russets for richness, Ashmead's Kernel for tannins, Calville Blanc for acidity

life story: fruit pressed late December, left outside to freeze; goes through two or three freeze–thaw cycles; mid-February, 8–10 week fermentation, arrested to ensure desired residual sugar

abv: 15%

if you like this: try Cinderella's Slipper, with dozens of old French varietals; Imperial 11° Rosé, juice co-fermented with redcurrants; Eden cans

experience: visit Eden Taproom, Newport, VT; Cider Week, Vermont & New York City; Franklin County CiderDays; Cider Summits; also check Facebook

edenciders.com

'I am not a dabbler.' That's a fair bit of self-analysis from the talented Eleanor Léger, the smiling driving force behind Eden. But then, if she hadn't persisted, ice ciders would have taken a while longer to arrive in the USA.

But we're getting ahead of ourselves. Eleanor landed with her husband, Albert, in Vermont in the mid-noughties, taking root in an abandoned farm near the Canadian borders. Witnessing what was going on north of the border with the Québec ice cider movement, Eleanor wondered: 'Why is no one doing that here?'

What started with 120 carboys evolved into a tussle to gain federal approval. Eleanor won and, in 2008, Vermont Ice Cider was born. Made using the cryoconcentration method, whereby the sweetness in the juice is concentrated prior to fermentation, this is a blend of 15 different heirloom varieties.

Intensely aromatic on the nose, with rich apricot and cling peach notes alongside a herbal hint, the palate is similarly intense. Tangerine zest amplifies the apricots and peaches. The acidity is perfectly poised, not too much and not too little.

Eden has a biodynamic orchard with 35 different varieties. An early *terroiriste* and eco-warrior, Eleanor's alliances with fellow orchardists in neighbouring regions are particularly important. Ten years ago, for example, they partnered with Scott Farms with its 120-variety strong orchard 270km (170 miles) away at the famed Landmark Trust property. Orchardist Ezekiel Goodband had grafted New England heirloom varieties onto the existing orchards. Through these collaborations, 'we have unique access to wonderful fruit,' says Eleanor.

'The key [for ice ciders] is having the acids,' she adds. And the right leader, I'd say.

eden
VERMONT ICE CIDER
HEIRLOOM
BLEND

FARNUM HILL
EXTRA DRY
CIDER
TRADITIONAL CIDERS FROM TRUE CIDER APPLES

FARNUM HILL
EXTRA DRY CIDER

Thank heaven for godchildren. Without them, Steve Wood and Louisa Spencer might not have been heading back to London from Chester in the early 1980s. 'We took the western route for the hell of it,' Steve says. 'Through Herefordshire, and I said "Look at the frickin' trees!"'

By then Steve already had over 15 years of orcharding under his belt, so the chance of an introduction to Bertram Bulmer, son of the founder of Bulmers, was accepted with alacrity. Bertram introduced him to pivotal orcharding individuals, people like the orchardist John Worle and the late Ray Williams, the latter from Long Ashton Research Station. There was no going back. Here was a world of different apples. These were tannin-rich varieties that conferred complexity and depth to a blend.

'I got curious about whether we could grow any of these apples,' he says. 'We grafted a few hundred varieties.' After extensive trials, 1989 saw 1,000 trees being planted. Eventually the whole of Poverty Lane Orchards became either cider fruit or heirlooms that work well in cider.

High-end, orchard-based ciders came next, just like the Extra Dry in my glass. It's the purity of fruit that stands out. We are in stone-fruit territory with the fragrance. The palate is elegant and rich, with peach notes, a herbal twang and lemony hints on the finish. There's a slight astringency, but overall the tannins have mellowed. A beautiful palate cleanser.

Over the years, dozens of cidermakers and orchardists have been inspired to follow Steve and Louisa's path. While much of cider is about the blend, as Steve says, 'Getting the right varieties is more important.' Too true.

region: Lebanon, New Hampshire, USA

fruit: a mix of predominantly cider varieties

life story: fermented slowly through to dryness in the cool New Hampshire climate; lengthy maturation and a rigorous blending process prior to bottling with gentle carbonation

abv: 7.5%

if you like this: seek out Farnum Hill's Kingston Black, Semi-Dry and its Cider Grown collaboration cans with Stormalong and Eden Specialty Cider

experience: keep an eye out on Facebook for news of Growler Days at Poverty Lane Orchards; join in the pick-your-own in the autumn

povertylane orchards.com

BIG HILL CIDERWORKS
GOLDEN RUSSET

region: Adams County, Pennsylvania, USA

fruit: Golden Russet, popular with growers and cidermakers alike for its complexity, rich flavours and good sugar potential

life story: apples left until fully ripe before harvesting; fermented slowly with natural yeasts through the winter; barrel-aged for a year before bottling

abv: 8.4%

if you like this: look for Barrel Aged Reserve; Thimbleberry in the Sour Series, wild fermented with raspberries and blackberries

experience: check out the Events page for local farmers' markets and other events

bighillcider.com

'We wait until they're dead ripe,' Troy Lehman tells me when I ask about the clarion-like call of his Golden Russet cider. That's been his and co-founder Ben Kishbaugh's take from the start. 'When you harvest those apples has everything to do with the fruit character, the taste, the fruit developing the character on the tree.

'We have the potential to develop an awesome product because of where Big Hill is,' says Troy. Acknowledging there are other areas where it is easier to grow 'pretty' apples, Big Hill, located near historic Gettysburg, is among the foothills of the Appalachian Mountains, and offers the soils and microclimate Troy and Ben want for their apples.

Troy and Ben set up Big Hill Ciderworks in 2014. Both refugees from the car industry, Troy grew up on a farm and Ben was an avid home-brewer. Together they have charge of 10ha (25 acres) of apples, with 40 different varieties, including cider classics such as Kingston Black, Dabinett and Stoke Red.

They are well known for their love of tannin-rich English and French varietals, so why have I got a Golden Russet in my glass?

'There's not that many heritage ciders that can be made from a single apple,' says Troy. While some in more northerly climes might find it difficult to get the ripeness necessary for complexity, Big Hill's environs obviously suit this one. And a year in ex-red-wine barrels has added another layer. Golden in the glass, this has honeyed notes, hints of vanilla, plus incredible depth and fragrance.

'When someone drinks a Big Hill cider, we want them to think of Big Hill,' says Troy. Job done, mate.

PROUDLY CRAFTED IN
ADAMS CO.
PENNA
Big Hill
CIDERWORKS
SMALL
BATCH
GOLDEN RUSSET
CIDER
GLUTEN FREE
8.4% ALC/VOL • 750 ML

ANXO
DISTRICT OF COLUMBIA

HAPPY TREES
SPONTANEOUSLY FERMENTED
DRY CIDER

ANXO
HAPPY TREES

ANXO's mission is to change the face of cider. Not just to educate, but to re-educate. Set up by Sam Fitz with his sister Rachel, and Cooper Sheehan, all craft-beer industry veterans, as well as breathing new life into the tree-to-table movement, they produce ciders with heart and heritage at their Cidery & Bar and across the city at their Cidery & Taproom.

Take Happy Trees: this uses fruit from a variety of orchards. Invariably a mix of heirloom and culinary varieties, it is produced batch by batch.

When we visited the Cidery & Bar, we tried Batch #3, a marriage of historic heirlooms Jonathan and Winesap with Virginia's classic, Albemarle Pippin. It's light and elegant, with a grapefruit zest infusion on the palate. Plus just the right amount of sparkle to bring out its almost wine-like nuanced flavours.

We also caught the tail end of #1, crafted from Arkansas Black, a fragrant, deep burgundy-coloured apple.

ANXO Cidery & Bar could be – or should be – the future. Wander in past apple trees, enter a bright bar with gleaming tap wall and 660-litre (174-gallon) oak barrel with black ribs and red-painted detail. Hailing from Barcelona, chef Alex Vallcorba serves up irresistible Basque-inspired *pintxos*. The classic cider pour and *porróns*, the traditional Spanish glass wine pitchers, are on offer too.

Chat with the staff, marvel at the extensive bottled cider list curated by Zach Dratch, or beg a space at the Tasting Bar upstairs. There are dozens of ciders on draught, or select a themed flight and settle down. The world of cider is moving and you're in the front seat.

region: Washington DC, USA

fruit: heirloom varieties Jonathan, Winesap, Albemarle Pippin

life story: spontaneous fermentation in 3,800-litre (1,000-gallon) barrels; ageing in ex-Sangiovese casks

abv: 6.7%

if you like this: try everything! Cidre Blanc, 100% Goldrush apples, Sauvignon Blanc yeast; Rosé; Collaboration Series, e.g. with Eden, Farnum Hill

experience: visit Cidery & Pintxos Bar, Truxton Circle, Washington DC; Cidery & Tasting Room, Brightwood Park, Wednesday–Sunday; follow social media

anxodc.com

SEA CIDER
KINGS & SPIES

region: Vancouver Island, British Columbia, Canada

fruit: native heirloom varieties; aromatic King of Tompkins, and American favourite, Northern Spy

life story: yeast selected to encourage acid-softening malolactic fermentation ('Island apples can be very acidic'); juice reserve added before bottling

abv: 8%

if you like this: try Perry, from a secret orchard; Pippins, made in the New England style; Wolf in the Woods, infused with hops and grand fir needles

experience: visit the Ciderhouse Tasting Room; buy an Artisan Lunch Plate to accompany a Tasting Flight; cyclists particularly welcomed; check out the Events calendar online

seacider.ca

Sociability, sustainability and community involvement: the three pillars upon which Kristen Needham has built SeaCider, the farm and cider house she opened to the public in 2007. A sixth-generation farmer, she hadn't intended to till the land, but with her original training being partly in environmental management, perhaps it was inevitable. Within a few years of returning home in 2002, she had planted over 1,000 trees with over 60 different varieties, including many from Europe.

Rather than Bittersweet or Flagship, her German-style cider, I've chosen Kings & Spies, where the fruit has all come from local gardens and orchards. It's a multi-faceted blend, but one with heritage, being based loosely on what the 19th century settlers would have bought with them when they arrived.

Pale, almost watery white in the glass, there's a persistent fine bead of bubbles. The fragrance mixes aromas from exotic white and wall-garden flowers. Light yellow fruits, green apple, white melon and fresh pear on a light-to-medium bodied palate, with light lemon notes on the finish.

A portion of proceeds goes to Growing Chefs, an initiative that educates local families about growing and preparing healthy food. So that's all three pillars covered: this cider involves the community, and is both sustainable and sociable. Ticks all round.

The Ciderhouse is firmly established on the tourist trail. I'll leave you with the last few lines from one of Kristen's poems:

Breathe deep and let your senses fill
Take in the sights from on our hill
Come raise a glass of cider here
Enjoy our farm, our view, our cheer

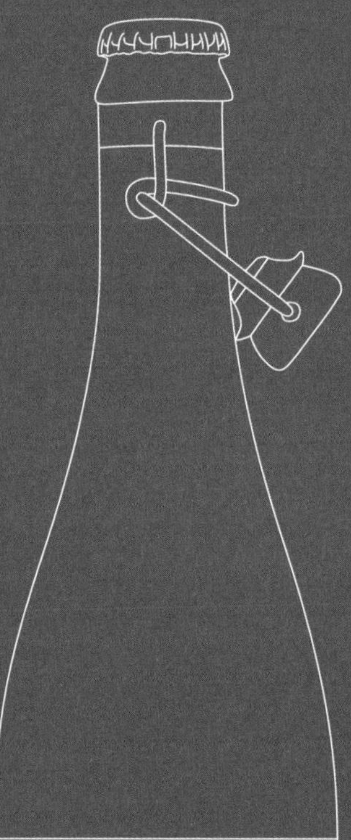

SEA CIDER
FARM & CIDERHOUSE
KINGS & SPIES
Heirloom Series
8% ALC./VOL.

CIDRERIE
LE

CIDRERIE LE SOMNAMBULE
LE SAUVAGE, 2017

The fragrance in my glass is captivating. What's the story here? How has this golden, hazy cider from the Québec region struck such a pose in this, the producers' debut vintage in charge?

Emile Robert's journey into cider is pretty unique. While researching the molecules present in apple aromas and their respective ciders for his PhD, he met renowned author and cider authority, Claude Jolicoeur. Claude introduced Emile to the practice of producing cider as well as the theory, and it wasn't long before Emile was part of the community. Once he began crafting his own cider, perhaps understandably, the lure of academia began to wane.

'One morning I typed "cideries for sale" into Google, not expecting anything,' he says. 'That's how we found Casa Breton. We planned a visit just for fun, knowing it was impossible for us youngsters to buy such a business.' His partner Eve soon joined the project, 18 months later the farm was theirs, and together they began Le Somnambule, The Sleepwalker.

From the start, it's a feast for the senses. First, there are the flowers, the sweet blossom and the warm citrus notes that cast a spell. There's lemon and grapefruit on the palate. Tart peach and unripe melon. It's fully dry, but with sweet fruit turning into orange, plus a hit of red apple and a lively sparkle.

Then there's the label – a moody, original wild cat image from Québec artist Michelle Larouche.

So why the name? 'We wanted a lot of freedom with our labels, and with The Sleepwalker we are in the realm of dreams and imagination,' he explains. 'So really, anything goes.'

region: Québec, Canada

fruit: Spartan and Jonamac, both dessert apples but chosen for their aromatics, from Casa Breton's orchards

life story: harvested mid-season. Low temperature, slow fermentation, natural yeast, multiple rackings before bottling with some residual yeast, so the cider conditions in bottle, adding to mouthfeel

abv: 6%

if you like this: try Le Céleste, Le Blanc de Pomme and Le Brut; look out for forthcoming natural fermentation ciders – 'It's what we want to develop more'

experience: take a guided tour and tasting; pick your own blueberries or apples

lesomnambule.com

CLOS SARAGNAT
AVALANCHE, 2014

region: Québec, Canada

fruit: unusual varieties, selected by Christian, farmed organically

life story: apples are picked while frozen, pressed straight away, the concentrated juice fermented for eight months, natural yeasts; left on lees for three years before bottling

abv: 9.5%

if you like this: try older vintages, like 2012

experience: visit Tasting Room, May–October, except Tuesdays; November–April, by appointment

saragnat.com

Christian Barthomeuf is the ice king. He pioneered ice cider years before it was recognised, helping today's market leaders hone their skills and launch their ranges. Having helped establish ice cider in the world's consciousness, he joined with Louise Dupuis, a fellow cidriculturist of note, and established Clos Saragnat.

There are two ways of making ice cider, cryoconcentration and cryoextraction. For both, Québec rules state that nature must do the freezing, not a cold store. Arguably the more challenging route, cryoextraction involves pressing frozen apples. Either harvest the apples as normal, store inside until temperatures are cold enough outside, or choose apple varieties that stay on the tree until the cold spells arrive. Then harvest and press immediately. That's what Christian and Louise do.

During pressing, the water ice crystals in the apple will get left behind since these are the last to thaw, and the juice emerges like an ambrosial nectar.

Waiting for the apples to freeze is tricky, both physically and logistically – imagine climbing a ladder in snowshoes. It's also risky because, even in cold climates like Québec, you can't rely on Arctic conditions every year. But Christian and Louise prefer it this way. It's the quality that matters.

The result? An incredible complexity of flavour, burnished copper in the glass, the aromas of caramel, toffee and nuts mix with a floral and herbal note. Textures of cooked apple, baked peach, tangerine and apricots mingle with candied fruit and raisins, and the vibrant acids lend an extremely long finish. A revelation.

DEPUIS
1989
SARAGNAT
CIDRE DE GLACE biologique ◊ Organic ICE CIDER
AVALANCHE
— RÉCOLTE HIVERNALE —
200 ml
9,5% alc. vol.

DU MINOT
DU MINOT
CIDRERIE

DES GLACES
CIDRE DE GLACE
Produit du Québec
ICE CIDER
Product of Quebec

CIDRERIE DU MINOT
DES GLACES, 2014

The Demoy family has been at this a while. In fact, Du Minot is the proud owner of Permit #1, dating from 1988, making it officially the first of the modern Canadian wave.

Hailing originally from Brittany, Robert and Joëlle arrived in the 1970s with a family cider history dating back over a century. At the time, Canada's cider reputation was not in a good place. Having been technically illegal until the early 1970s – it was 'forgotten' when the 1921 legislation was passed – initially the market was flooded with poor ciders.

Robert, with his University of Bordeaux training, was originally hired to help a winery. In late 1986, the law changed, allowing artisan drinks production. Very soon, the Demoys bought their 51-ha (126-acre) site, with a 7-ha (17-acre) orchard. Two years later, they released their first cider.

Their family – daughter Audrenne and son Alan – are now at the helm. Now with 24ha (59 acres) of orchards, Du Minot draws on 20 different varieties, from popular North American heirlooms such as McIntosh through to modern, hardy apples like Cortland.

Du Minot is part of Cidre du Québec, meaning that they can only cryoconcentrate (see page 220) using natural cold rather than a cold store. This long, slow process produces a sublime cider of incredible richness.

There's baked apple with demerara on the nose, cooked peach, tangerine and a herbal hint. Burnished gold in colour, the palate is very ripe, with yellow dessert apple notes underlaid with cooked apricots. Beautiful acidity provides the perfect counterpoint.

One other claim to fame, Robert invented the word 'cidriculturist', for the cidermaker who tends his or her own orchards. Seems rather appropriate.

region: Québec, Canada

fruit: a blend of McIntosh, Cortland, Empire, Liberty, Trent

life story: apples are harvested, stored in a fridge, pressed when it is -10°C (14°F) outside; water separates out when the tank thaws; nectar drawn off, for eight-month fermentation

abv: 10%

if you like this: try Crémant de Pomme; Crémant du Glace, as with Des Glaces, plus secondary *charmat* fermentation

experience: Le Mondial des Cidres, Montreal, March; visit Cidrerie: April–December, all week; January–March, Monday–Friday; group tours on application; vintage equipment museum

duminot.com

DOMAINE DES SALAMANDRES
POIRÉ DE GLACE, 2013

region: Covey Hill, Québec, Canada

fruit: Bartlett, Bosc and Flemish Beauty pears

life story: when temperature reaches -10°C (14°F), pears are pressed, juice freezes outside; thawed concentrated juice ferments for eight months

abv: 10%

if you like this: try Limited Edition, aged for two years in oak barrels

experience: visit May–Sep, see website for hours; see Facebook for events; look up Circuit du Paysan (lecircuitdupaysan), for fellow artisan producers

salamandres.ca

Imagine moving your young family to the scenic surroundings of the Adirondack foothills, planting thousands of vines, then three years later having half of the vines wiped out by a cruel frost. That's what happened to Denise Lavoie and Sylvain Haut when they settled in Covey Hill, the beautiful region straddling the US-Canadian border.

Rather than give up, however, they not only replanted but put in 300 pear trees. Choosing three varieties – Bosc, Bartlett and Flemish Beauty – this time they decided to let nature take the lead, but in a beneficial rather than a destructive way, by focusing on *poiré de glace*, ice perry. Sylvain had worked at Domaine Neige, one of the region's pioneers.

Temperatures in this region plummet in the winter. To get the sugar-rich juice needed for ice perry fermentation, Domaine des Salamandres uses cryoconcentration. Freshly pressed juice is left outside to freeze. (Elsewhere, where temperatures aren't so extreme, juice tanks are frozen indoors.) When the days begin to warm up, the sugar-rich juice is the first to melt, and this is drawn off to begin its fermentation.

We have the original here – there's also a barrel-aged version. Bronze gold in colour, this has incredible depth on the nose, with apricots, peaches, kumquats, and tangerine zest. The palate is similarly intense, with zesty oranges, fresh cling peaches and tart apricots. There's a good balancing acidity, with a sweet citrus note on the finish. And yes, as the experts suggest, this does indeed go with blue cheese!

And the name? Covey Hill is one of the world's last refuges for the tiny mountain dusky salamander. Nature providing inspiration once more.

POIRÉ DE GLACE
ICE PERRY

DOMAINE DES SALAMANDRES

VIN DE POIRE | PEAR WINE

200 ml 10 % alc./vol.

AUSTRALIA, NEW ZEALAND & SOUTH AFRICA

If these are the youngest cider – and perry – producers in our book, they are also among the most dynamic, having a true sense of purpose coupled with an infectiously energetic approach.

Apples and pears grow best in the Southern Hemisphere between the latitudes of 30° and 45°. There is no 'one style fits all' in this brave new cider world. Traditional-method sparkling ciders sit alongside keeved ciders. Still ciders rub alongside carbonated.

While hotter climates might favour easy drinking, refreshment-style ciders, these wine-literate nations are also open to embracing the smaller serve. Knowing the value of provenance and flavour brings with it an appreciation of the more orchard-driven, *terroir*-related ciders. With that, as elsewhere, comes a respect and desire for bittersweet and bittersharp apple varieties to complement the culinary and dessert apples doing so well in these climates.

In **Australia**, orchards are established in all states bar the Northern Territory, with Victoria and Tasmania being the most densely populated. Indeed, Tasmania used to be known as the Apple Isle.

EXPLORE

Cider Australia: cideraustralia.org.au

Cider NZ: cidernz.com

Australian Cider Festival, October, ciderfestival.com.au

Huon Valley Mid-Winter Fest, July: valleymidwinterfest.com.au

Kellybrook Cider Festival, May: kellybrookwinery.com.au/festival

New Zealand Cider Festival, November: nzciderfestival.com

The Cider Link: theciderlink.com.au

With Britain's entry into the European Common Market in the 1970s, Tasmania's main export market all but disappeared, causing shockwaves around the island. Not all growers survived, but among those who did was Willie Smith's.

Back on the mainland, visionary individuals like the late Drew Henry indelibly left their mark. Realising something was missing, he kicked matters off in the 1990s at Henry of Harcourt, bringing in bittersweet and bittersharp apple varieties.

The last decade has seen much development. Cider Australia, established in 2012, with its outward-looking approach as well as its quality-focused mantra, is proving an effective producer association.

Modern-day pioneers include Willie Smith's Tim Jones, who happily mixes traditional techniques with insight brought over from the wine industry. Others, like James Kendell of Small Acres, New South Wales, are part of the growing band happy to craft poised blends from myriad cider and dessert apple varieties.

Meanwhile, across the Tasman Sea, **New Zealand** is working with its own potent blend of enviable growing conditions wrapped up with an enthusiastic quest for clarity and complexity. Growing is focused around Hawke's Bay in the North Island and the Nelson region in the South Island, cider varieties are joining the dessert and culinary plantings, and the open-mindedness of both consumer and maker shines through. Alex Peckham is among those pioneering bittersweet fruit as well as trying the French keeving process (see page 221), while Zeffer keeps environmental sustainability close to its heart.

South Africa is the true baby of the craft cidermaking bunch. While the Western Cape has been known for decades for the quality of its dessert apples, only recently has craft cider begun to make its mark. Our representative, the energetic Sxollie, draws its fruit from Elgin Valley, responsible for over half the Rainbow Nation's apple crop. Interestingly, the soft drink Appletiser has its roots in Elgin Valley back in the 1960s. Perhaps the region will bear witness to the rise of South Africa's craft industry too.

WILLIE SMITH'S KINGSTON BLACK, 2017

Limited Release

region: Huon Valley, Tasmania, Australia

fruit: Kingston Black, one of the world's classic cider varietals

life story: hand harvested; three different yeasts to conserve aromatics; fermented through to dryness. Kingston Black juice added back to taste, carbonated

abv: 6.2%

if you like this: try 23 Varieties, made with 23 different French and British bittersweets; Traditional Cider; Organic Cider; Farmhouse Perry

experience: visit Apple Shed, Apple Museum, check website for music, food, cider and community events; Huon Valley Mid-Winter Festival; The Tasmanian Cider Trail

williesmiths.com.au

With its equitable climate and rich patchwork of soils, until about 50 years ago Tasmania was known as the Apple Isle. Then the global market hit the buffers. One family business determined to survive was Willie Smith's. Through grit and good sense, Ian and Dianne Smith fought their way through.

One game-changer came when son Andrew persuaded them to go organic. The next, in 2012, a century after the first commercial cider was produced on the island, Willie Smith's released its own cider.

Today 22ha (55 acres) are home to 25 different apples, including several English and French cider varieties, and Willie Smith's is in the vanguard of the new face of Australian cidermaking. As I write, cider business co-founder and MD Sam Reid is president of Cider Australia, and its Kingston Black sparkling cider has just been crowned Reserve Champion at the Royal Bath & West International Cider Championship. 'Our approach is a hybrid,' says head cidermaker Tim Jones. 'It's a mixture of quite traditional with New World know-how.'

This is illustrated beautifully by the 2017 Kingston Black. For an apple that inspires one and all but is notoriously difficult to work with, here's a seemingly effortless attempt. To achieve this, behind the scenes, among other things, Tim has focused real attention on capturing the aromatics. Ripe autumnal apple scents mix with the warmth of the sun. A rich, warm gold in colour, the palate has a delicate sparkle and very fine tannins. Yellow and red apple flavours mix with apricot and peach notes, while tangerine zest accentuates a lengthy finish.

While Tim has his own 'hobby' orchard at home to carry on the explorations, Sam's quest is for Tasmania to be known as the Cider Isle. Good idea.

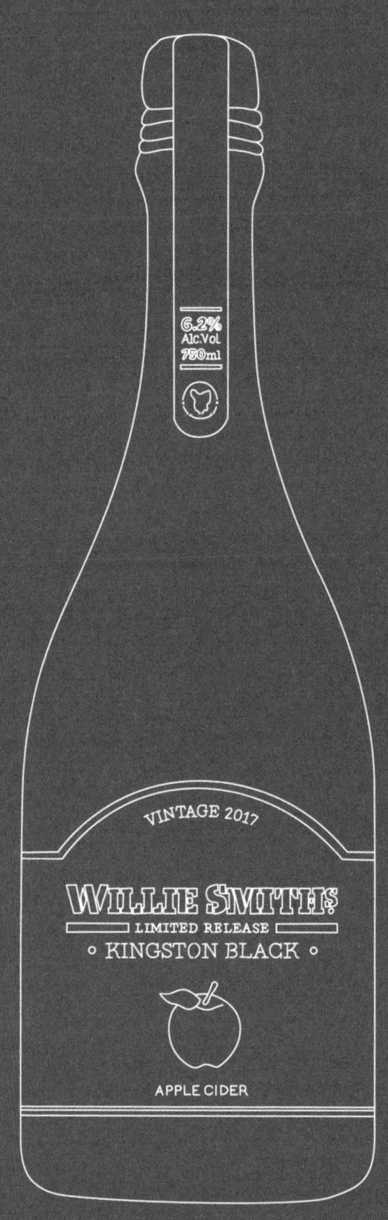
6.2%
Alc.Vol.
750ml
VINTAGE 2017
WILLIE SMITH'S
LIMITED RELEASE
KINGSTON BLACK
APPLE CIDER

St. Ronan's
METHODE TRADITIONALE
APPLE CIDER
YARRA VALLEY
750mL

ST RONAN'S
APPLE CIDER, HERITAGE FRUIT

'As a kid, we have seen lots of orchards being knocked down and planted to vineyards but now it's swinging back again,' says Troy Jones, co-founder of St Ronan's, the cider producer making waves with its *méthodes traditionelles* – MTs – in the Yarra Valley. 'Yarra is a cool climate region. There are hundreds of orchards around here,' he says. 'Lots of specific microclimates and distinct soil types.' St Ronan's is helping to harness this, putting Yarra on the cider world map.

Troy and his 'much better half' Bec love the MT style of sparkling cider. Charcuterie-makers, it proved the perfect partner. 'We just loved the level of complexity, fruit, tannin and acid,' he says. When they couldn't find what they wanted locally, 'We said F#@k it, let's make our own!'

Come in long-time friend Eric Driessen. A talented blueberry grower and winemaker, his family had been hit badly by the 2009 fires, and so was open to a new challenge. Blueberries still continue but since 2010, cider and perry have loomed large too. Recognition came soon, with the Best Australian Perry award at the 2012 Cider Australia awards.

While Eric's family have been successful growers for decades, Troy has winemaking experience, including a line of wine, Payten & Jones, with friend Behn Payten. St Ronan's range now includes stubbies, kegged cider, and perhaps most excitingly the Heritage Fruit line, including apples from Troy and Bec's new cider-variety-tinged orchards.

Deep, burnished gold in the glass, there's exotic stone fruit on the nose, with apricots and warm peaches. On the palate, the tang of tart apricot and peach leads, along with mandarin zest, to good balancing acids and a light sparkle. Now where's that salami...

Méthode Traditionelle

region: Yarra Valley, South Australia

fruit: a blend of Kingston Black, Golden Harvey, Improved Foxwhelp, Yarlington Mill, Bulmer's Norman; the first MT from St Ronan's own orchard

life story: first fermentation in the tank followed by a secondary fermentation in the bottle, with time spent on lees before disgorging and bottling

abv: 10.5%

if you like this: try Pear Cider; Apple Cider

experience: head to Cellar Door at Blueberry Farm, Healesville, Thursday–Monday; Wine & Wildlife, Healesville Sanctuary, June; follow Facebook for details of events

stronanscider.com.au

HENRY OF HARCOURT
DUCK & BULL

region: Harcourt, Victoria, Australia

fruit: a blend of 43 traditional French and cider varieties with Pink Lady dessert apple, harvested from February through May

life story: majority of apples blended pre-fermentation, with key varieties, fermented separately; sparkling wine yeast; fermentation through to dryness; *dosage* of yeast/sugar added for bottle conditioning

abv: 8.4%

if you like this: try the legendary champion, Kingston Black; Gylden Pære, four-perry pear blend

experience: visit the Cellar Door, open all year; pressing demos at cidery during Harcourt Apple Fest, Australian Cider Festival; follow social media

henrycider.com

The fact that the name on the bottle includes the words 'orchardists & cidermakers' gives you a clue that these folk truly respect the apple. Not for them the concentrate-laden fizzy pop that oft masquerades as cider.

With characteristic verve and vigour, Australia is tackling the *terroiriste* view of cider. One of the undoubted pioneers was Drew Henry, so the news of his untimely death in 2017 caused a shockwave throughout the cider world.

Back in the 1990s, Drew and his wife swapped a geologist's life for one in the orchard. They landed in Harcourt, 90 minutes north of Melbourne, a premium apple-growing region. Drew and his son Michael began making cider in the 1990s, and, from the start, their appreciation of the place and value of cider fruit shone through.

Today, the Henry family, who luckily for us decided to keep Henry of Harcourt going, grows over 40 different varieties of apples and pears. Daughter-in-law Troy has joined the crew, boasting the best job title, Pommelier and Cider Pirate, and with her assistance, I tried Duck & Bull.

Showing vivid apple notes throughout, it begins with autumnal Russet aromas with a tangerine hint; the palate is expressive and streamlined, while well-judged bottle conditioning carries the flavour through.

And the name? That's Nicole the mother duck and Zenith the champion bull. After a few run-ins, they became the best of friends. Much, the Henrys say, like this blend of dessert and cider apples. Not an obvious marriage. But boy, doesn't it work well.

I wouldn't chill this cider. Rather savour every element. And raise a glass to a true legend. Drew, your ciders have done your orchards proud. Wassail.

HENRY OF
HARCOURT
ORCHARDISTS & CIDERMAKERS
DUCK &
BULL
Bottle Conditioned
Made from 100% Real Apples
Product of Australia
500 ml

LOBO

LOBO
NORMAN, 2014

It's not often you see a cider bottle with a fox with a 'tache riding a bicycle. But then this is Lobo. This is what happens when a fifth-generation apple grower teams up with a Somerset cidermaker with the freedom of the Adelaide Hills as the backdrop.

Michael Stafford is the orchardist, and ex-Brit Warwick Billings has been making cider since he was in shorts. Warwick originally landed in Australia to learn about wine science, intending to return to cidermaking in Blighty, but somehow that never happened.

What about our friend the louche wolf? As well as being the Spanish for wolf, Lobo is the name of a desirable dessert apple. Each label embodies what's in the bottle. This one is Norman, so our friend appears to be taking us on his own Tour de France.

What a treat! Whiffs of smoke meld with warm, yellow apple on the nose. Burnished gold in the glass, there's a tantalising hisssssssss as this is opened. Warwick has shared with me one of the last 2014s – the 2017s are still conditioning. This is very lightly cloudy, as are all the Lobo ciders. Deliberately so. 'No filtering, no pasteurising,' Warwick says determinedly.

Scoring Gold at Cider Australia a few years ago, the palate carries on the burnished character. Very fine tannins, this is without doubt dry, with flavours of Russet and warm autumn leaves. There's a sassy lick of citrus, plus green, tart apples and the bitter zest of Seville orange on the finish.

'We're on a bit of a mission to show people the range and depth of ciders that can be made from apples,' says Warwick. Mission accomplished, I'd say.

region: Lenswood, South Australia

fruit: a blend of English cider varieties, including classics Kingston Black, Dabinett and Yarlington Mill, with crab apples, plus dessert varieties, including Pink Lady and Golden Delicious

life story: fermented, bottled after nine months with a little yeast for second fermentation; not disgorged

abv: 6.9%

if you like this: try Cloudy Apple; Perry; Royale; Lobodos Apple Brandy

experience: Cider Sunday once a month at Adelaide Showground Farmers' Market; available throughout Australia; follow social media for details of events

loboapple.com

DAYLESFORD
SWEET COPPIN, 2017

region: Near Melbourne, Victoria, Australia

fruit: traditional sweet and bittersweet blend, including the fruit-forward Sweet Coppin

life story: apples are harvested relatively late; fermentation is long and cool, with selected yeast strains; backsweetened with Granny Smith/Pink Lady juice

abv: 4.4%

if you like this: try alf' n alf', a blend inspired by a visit to Julian Temperley at Burrow Hill, Somerset; French Oak, bottle conditioned with English cider varieties

experience: Tavern Cellar Door open all week; drop by the English-style Tavern, buy a paddle of cider; check out events calendar for live music updates

daylesfordcider.com.au

That's bold – a naturally sweet, still cider. A palate with ripe, baked apples, cling peaches and honey, and thick-cut marmalade. Fullbodied, there's just enough acid to balance the rich fruit, with astringency coming from the tannins nestling within the basket of almost Russet-/Cox-like sweetness.

But then Clare and Jon Mackie – Mackie to his mates – are happy doing things differently. Before they bought Daylesford Cider near Melbourne three years ago, they had set up a veggie burger business in Darwin because of 'a lack of healthy vego/vegano options', Clare tells me. She's an ex-pat Brit, with a three-year stint in Bristol – self-styled City of Cider – to her name. And a liking for 'real' cider.

They had been talking about making cider and setting up a café. 'Mackie has a background in farming and environmental science and was also up for a new challenge,' Clare says.

In the early 2010s, they noticed Daylesford Cider, it being one of very few orchards in Australia growing traditional English cider apples. 'Little did we know he was looking to retire!' says Clare, with a laugh.

Within a few years of being in the Mackies' care, Daylesford caught the limelight at the Australian Cider Awards, winning Best in Category for its Sweet Coppin. While named in honour of the fruit-forward Sweet Coppin, originally from Somerset, this is actually a blend, with 18 other varieties, including Kingston Black, Brown Snout and Alford Sweet.

'The heritage varieties for us are important as they are traditional, cider apples. Ones used for generations with fantastic results,' says Clare. They're in good hands now, too.

DAYLESFORD
CIDER
EST 2003
HANDCRAFTED IN DAYLESFORD, VICTORIA
USING ORGANICALLY GROWN HERITAGE APPLES
SWEET COPPIN
4.4% ALC/VOL
330ML

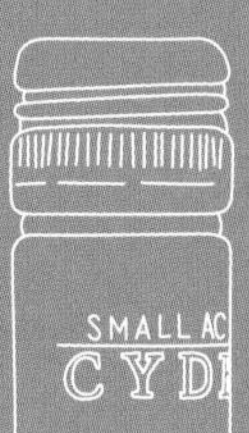
SMALL ACRES
CYDE

SMALL ACRES
CYDER
Norfolk Still
2016
TRADITIONAL MEDIUM DRY
ALCOHOLIC CIDER
ORANGE NSW

SMALL ACRES CYDER
NORFOLK STILL, 2016

It's when the birds arrive that James Kendell, co-founder of Small Acres, starts thinking about harvesting. When they start pecking at the apples, James knows they're getting ripe. 'I start to eat them,' he says. 'So it's by taste first and then I break out the equipment and measure the Baumé.' Instinct plus high-tech know-how for Small Acres, the cidery established by James and his wife Gail in the mid-noughties.

Gail grew up in Bristol, surrounded by English cider country. James worked for Courage, the brewers, in the UK, at the time when they owned a cider brand. Probably equally important, he travelled – France, Spain, also Germany. 'I got exposed to all those different (cider) styles and the culture,' he says.

After they returned to Australia it wasn't long before the lure of the land and the obvious dearth of cider with character took hold. James had grown up on a sheep farm. 'I always wanted to go back to the country,' he says.

They scouted out the regions, deciding upon Orange, about 270km (168 miles) west of Sydney. At nearly 1,000m (3,330ft) above sea level, although the days get hot, the evenings cool down, offering good ripening conditions.

And that ripeness comes through on the Norfolk Still. It's 7% and yet it's medium in sweetness, with no added sugar. Just the adoption of winemaking techniques (see life story).

Gloriously clear and yellow gold in colour, this is fragrant, with aromas of acacia and ripe, bruised apples. The apple flavours continue all the way through, broadening to include red and yellow plus a tinge of green adding contrast. A honeyed hint sits alongside peach and ripe apricot. No wonder the birds were happy.

region: Orange, New South Wales, Australia

fruit: 13 cider varieties, including classics like Kingston Black and Stoke Red, make up 20%; dessert apples, mainly Pink Lady and Granny Smith

life story: harvested and pressed immediately; stainless steel fermentation with wine yeast for 7–10 days; once it reaches the desired abv, cold crashed and sterile filtered to remove yeast but retain natural sweetness, as happens in winemaking

abv: 7%

if you like this: try The Cat's Pyjamas; Sparkling Perry; Pomona Ice

experience: Cellar Door, weekends; match ciders with lunch from the regional produce fridge; join the Cyder Club; follow social media

smallacrescyder.com.au

ABEL
MÉTHODE CIDER, 2016

region: Nelson, New Zealand

fruit: blend of heritage varieties such as Cox's Orange Pippin and Sturmer, with cider varieties including Kingston Black, Gravenstein and Bisque

life story: the varieties are fermented separately, using a mix of natural and artificial yeasts; unfined and unfiltered, the fermentation finishes in the bottle

abv: 6.5%

if you like this: pair with sustainably farmed salmon; or steam green-lipped mussels. 'Yummo,' says Mark

experience: find in New Zealand and parts of Australia; follow Facebook for details of tastings

abelcider.com

Everyone knows the clarity and vivacity of Marlborough Sauvignon Blanc. The piercing green fruits and punchy acidity. Well, translate that to the cider world and you're getting near to the electrifying effect of Abel's Méthode Cider.

Citrus aromas of depth and breadth continue onto the palate, where they open up to become lime and lemon with hints of orange zest. There's a definite green apple tang – no yellow apple flavours here.

But where does that piercing quality come from? Founders Mark and Sophie McGill both hail from winemaking backgrounds, and that's certainly played a part. Their young family brought them back to New Zealand, where they both grew up. Now they combine the worlds of cider and wine. The fruit is grown in orchards in the north-western corner of the South Island, named after the local Abel Tasman Park.

'It's about taking care of the fruit, which we treat with kid gloves,' Mark tells me. And taking a big hit on yields because of their unique way of fermenting their cider. Instead of pressing the pulp before fermenting, they press after, reckoning this way they will achieve the maximum flavours, aromas and intensity from the skins. 'We don't know anyone else making cider like this. Probably because it does cut your yields significantly,' says Mark. They achieve around 500 litres (132 gallons) from a tonne of fruit, rather than the more normal 750 litres (200 gallons).

It took seven years to perfect Méthode Cider. Mark continues to experiment every vintage, with new varieties and new techniques. 'Maybe in three to five years we will have another cider', he says. '... maybe!'

ABEL
MÉTHODE CIDER

RARE NELSON CIDER
PECKHAM'S
CIDERY & ORCHARD
SWEET SERIOUS
FRENCHIE
ANCIENT CRAFT • WILD FERMENT

PECKHAM'S CIDERY & ORCHARD

SWEET SERIOUS FRENCHIE

'I think *terroir* for apples is going to become really important.' That's Alex Peckham addressing the throng at 2018 CiderCon in Baltimore. As one of the pioneers of orchard-based cider in New Zealand who's also not afraid to experiment – cider with feijoa fruit anyone? – he's among friends. And he's also staked the family business on this.

Alex and Caroline arrived in New Zealand in the early noughties from England. He's a geologist, she's a linguist, and they have a shared passion for environmental matters.

Missing cider, they opted to make their own. Wanting some tannic structure, they were the first to plant cider varietals in New Zealand, and that's where the ongoing research began. A few years later they moved to Moutere Valley, near Nelson. 'True apple country,' they say, pointing at the clay soils and 'exceptional' sunlight hours.

Now they have 7ha (17 acres) of apple trees, with 30 different varieties. 'It's mainly West-Country varieties,' Alex says, 'although I really like French and Spanish varieties too.' There's also talk of more regrafting.

Sweet Serious Frenchie is Peckham's first attempt at keeving, the process perfected by the French which enables the final cider to retain a level of sweetness rather than, as apples will naturally do, ferment all the way through to dryness.

There is a beautiful balance, with just the right amount of acid to counterpoint delicate, apple snow flavours and to dance alongside the ripe but gentle tannins.

Winners of more silverware than a young cidery has a right to, Alex's hunch about *terroir* looks like coming true.

region: Moutere Valley, Nelson, New Zealand

fruit: a pre-fermentation blend of the best late season bittersweet varieties, including Browns, Harry Master's Jersey, Stoke Red and Knotted Kernel

life story: the juice undergoes the keeving process, is slowly fermented using wild yeast, aged for six months in tank before lightly carbonating, canning or bottling

abv: 4.8%

if you like this: try Moutere Cider and Perry, the house offer; Reserve Dry; Two Barrel Perry; Boysenberry

experience: New Zealand Cider Festival, Nelson; check Facebook for events and tastings; available in USA

peckhams.co.nz

ZEFFER
CIDRE DEMI-SEC, 2015

region: Hawke's Bay, New Zealand

fruit: a selection of over 50 English and French cider varieties

life story: fresh pressed juice undergoes a natural keeving process before natural fermentation with multiple racking; aged for about six months in old wine barrels prior to bottling

abv: 4.5%

if you like this: try the original, Crisp Apple; Hopped; Apple Crumble Infused; Slack Ma Girdle

experience: available in Australia, Thailand, China and elsewhere in Asia; follow Facebook for events news; Tasting Room opening late 2018

zeffer.co.nz

Moving a cidery 500km (300 miles) and only losing one day's work is no mean feat. Particularly when it's more than one press and one apple mill. And Zeffer has certainly gone beyond that. What began in a shed in Matakana, north of Auckland, in 2009 is about to surpass the million-litre (264,000-gallon) mark, has smashed one crowdfunding target – as I write, there's another on the go – and made inroads into China.

It all began when Matakana farmers' market regulars took a shine to the ciders being conjured up by local winemaker Sam Whitmore in his spare time. Fellow co-founder Hannah Bower saw the potential, and Josh Townsend, inspired by tastes at the market, soon joined the crew.

The fourth member to the party is Jody Scott, an ex-Brit with West Country cidermaking credentials. Arriving via Normandy, Adelaide and California, Jody is Sam's partner in crime as they craft ciders with texture and vibrancy.

New World technique happily meets Old World traditions in their range. Cidre Demi-Sec illustrates this: full-on cider apples, naturally keeved to retain sweetness.

Rich Russet meets warm apple notes on the nose. It's quite something on the palate too. Medium to full bodied, medium in sweetness, there's baked apple with demerara sugar crossed with *tarte tatin* flavours. A friendly sparkle plus slight hints of thick-cut marmalade lead to a long, rounded, honeyed finish. They recommend *crêpes suzette*. I'd say cheese, whether blue, Comté or Camembert.

They are sustainability pioneers – waste water is used to irrigate local orchards and lucky cows get the unwanted pomace. And destined for their reserve range is fruit from 1,500 recently planted cider-apple trees. Watch this space.

PREMIUM CRAFT

CIDRE DEMI-SEC

2015

French Traditional

Medium sweet cider. 100% cider apples. Wild fermentation, naturally keeved to retain natural sweetness. Elegantly balanced with rich tannin and subtle oak character.

NEW ZEALAND

SXOLLIE
CRIPPS PINK
CRAFT CIDER

SXOLLIE
CRIPPS PINK

'I always talk about a revolution because what we need to demonstrate is that, just like craft beer came to challenge the SABs (South African Breweries) of this world, craft cider is better able to create handcrafted, more evolved cider.' So says Karol Ostaszewksi in the South African *Craft Cider Revolution* video, explaining how he and fellow founder and partner, Laura Clacey, set up Sxollie.

'I was in a nightclub and they were playing this song here in Cape Town, "Everyday I'm hustling... I'm hustling, I'm hustling,"' he says. 'It's exactly the story of living in South Africa... every day you've got to work through absolutely everything to make something operate.' Come in 'Sxollie', taken from 'scallywag' in English and 'skorrie-morrie' in Afrikaans.

But Sxollie isn't just words. The pair headed to the valleys – Elgin, in particular, a cool region renowned for crystalline Sauvignon Blancs. They partnered with Fruitways Farming, kicking off their ciders with Golden Delicious, says Laura, 'because it's Africa's darling apple.' Next came the snappier Granny Smith followed by Packham Pear. The fruit flavours are ripe – you can taste the apple you are drinking – but the balancing acids are there too, alongside a well-judged sparkle.

The latest, Cripps Pink, is not pink but uses the eponymous apple. Needing a long growing season, South Africa is ideal, and Sxollie's wine-like production methods preserve its fragrance perfectly. It's fresh, exuding youthful apple fruit flavours and sweetness.

Karol and Laura returned to the roots of their brand with Cripps Pink. A percentage of profits go to Self Help Africa. 'We're doing our bit to help hustle for women in agriculture,' Karol tells me. Now that's revolutionary.

region: Elgin, South Africa

fruit: Cripps Pink, better known by its trademark name, Pink Lady, the offspring of Golden Delicious and Lady Williams

life story: harvested and cold-stored until time to press; cold-pressed, then, unusually, fermentation takes place with skins and pulp, adding to flavour/tannin, temperature controlled in stainless steel; blended back with fresh juice to sweeten

abv: 4.5%

if you like this: try Golden Delicious, Packham Pear, Granny Smith, or ciders from fellow South Africans Cluver & Jack, and Everson's

experience: available in South Africa, UK, USA, Singapore, Hong Kong, Namibia, Botswana; follow Facebook

sxolliecider.com

GLOSSARY

backsweetening – prior to bottling, a dry cider can be sweetened with sugar, artificial sweetener or apple/pear juice
biennialism – a tree that produces a bounty of crop one year and very little the next. Cider-apple trees can be very susceptible to this trait, although pruning and fruit thinning often helps
bottle conditioning – like traditional method, a small amount of yeast and sugar added post-fermentation to induce secondary fermentation in the bottle and provide natural sparkle, without riddling and disgorging. *See* sparkling cider box
chapeau brun – *see* keeving
***charmat* method** – the secondary fermentation occurs under pressure in a tank; the resulting sparkling cider is filtered and bottled under pressure; *see* sparkling cider box

SPARKLING CIDER

By far the most common method of making a cider sparkle is force carbonation, but there are a number of more sophisticated methods.
Pét-nat, (*pétillant naturel*), aka *méthode ancestrale*: partially fermented juice is bottled just before the sugars have all been used; the remaining yeast ferments the sugars, producing and trapping carbon dioxide in the process.

Secondary bottle fermentation, known as traditional or champagne method: the juice finishes fermenting; the new cider is bottled with yeast and sugar; fermentation takes place and cider is left on the lees for a time, depending on the style of cider wanted. The riddling process collects dead yeast cells prior to disgorging; a bottle is gently rotated each day, moving from a horizontal to a vertical position. Opening the bottle, pent-up pressure from the fermentation swiftly expels the yeast plug, the bottle is topped up/sweetened to taste (the ***dosage***) and recapped/corked.

See also ***charmat*; bottle conditioning; transfer method**

FROM BUD TO BOTTLE – A BRIEF GUIDE TO MAKING CIDER

Making cider and perry is a succession of choices. First, when and how – windfall collection, panking, light tree-shaking, ladder – to harvest. Each variety ripens at a different time. Sugar and starch tests are the simplest to perform. Fruit can be milled immediately or left to ripen further for a few weeks, depending on variety (apples and pears ripen off the tree). Fruit is washed and sorted before milling, then the pulp can be left to macerate for a few days or pressed straight away via a basket, rack and cloth, belt or pneumatic press. The juice is pumped to a fermentation vessel: a barrel, plastic IBC or stainless steel tank. Fermentation, which may be temperature controlled, is via natural yeast – from the air, within the apple and on its skin – or a cultured yeast.

Spent pomace can be spread throughout the orchard, used as animal feed or for an anaerobic digester.

Yeast and sugar levels are monitored throughout. Unlike perry, which has some unfermentable sugars, all sugars in apples are fermentable so apple juice will ferment to dryness unless the cidermaker intervenes. Once fermentation has finished, new cider is **racked** off its dead yeast cells – the **lees** – and can be **matured** in tank, barrel or IBC before bottling, canning, kegging, or filling into bag-in-box. Cidermakers can choose to filter, pasteurise or carbonate. Dry ciders can be **backsweetened** to become medium or sweet as well as dry. Ciders can be still or sparkling.
See also **keeving**; **sparkling cider box**

cold crashing – dropping temperature rapidly towards end of fermentation to 'knock' yeast out and stop fermentation; the new cider might still be pasteurised or sterile filtered to ensure stability
cryoconcentration/cryoextraction – two methods whereby sugars in apple/pear juice are concentrated, giving ice cider/perry, with an intense, tangy sweetness

culín – two fingers' worth of cider, the common measure when an *escanciador* pours Asturian *sidra natural*
disgorging – *see* sparkling cider box
dosage – topping up after disgorging a traditional method sparkling cider; the *dosage* sweetness dictates final cider sweetness; *see also* sparkling cider box
espalmé – the way carbon dioxide is released when an *escanciador* pours *sidra natural*; a sign of quality; *see pegue*
Euskal Sagardoa – *see* stamps of quality
filtration – removing insoluble particles and/or bacteria before bottling
keeving – process perfected in Britanny and Normandy ensuring juice stops fermenting before all sugars have been consumed, leaving natural sweetness. Happens naturally, but often an enzyme and calcium salt are added at start, causing a brown gel-like substance (the *chapeau brun)* to form, capturing some yeast and their nutrients, and floating to top. Juice underneath is racked into other tank continuing slow fermentation, stopping short of full dryness
lagar/llagar – name for cider cellar/s in Asturias, where the cider is made; also the name for the mill
lees – dead yeast cells
malolactic fermentation – the process whereby tangy malic acid is converted to softer, lactic acid; occurs naturally after first fermentation or can be induced
maturation – period post-fermentation whereby cider continues to evolve, in tank or bottle, before being released
PDO/PGI – *see* stamps of quality
pegue – the lacing left on a glass when an *escanciador* has poured a *sidra natural*; a sign of quality
pét-nat – *see* sparkling cider box
pome – a type of fruit produced by flowering plants, part of the rose family. Apples, pears and quinces are the best known pome fruits
racking – transferring cider from one vessel to another by pump or gravity
riddling – *see* sparkling cider box
secondary fermentation – yeast and sugar added to freshly fermented cider/perry to provide natural sparkle and/or further complexity; *see* sparkling wine
sidra natural/sagardo naturala – natural cider in Spanish/Basque

STAMPS OF QUALITY

Some regions have **PDO** (Protected Designation of Origin), **AOP** (Appellation d'Origine Protegée) or **PGI** (Protected Geographical Indication) status for their ciders/perries. To achieve this, a set of regulations governing provenance, fruit type, and sometimes production methods are put in place, along with tests for producers to pass to allow them to display the logo.

ENGLAND: Herefordshire, Gloucestershire, Worcestershire – perry and cider PGI. FRANCE: Two cider PDOs: Pays d'Auges, Cornouaille; one perry AOP: Domfront. SPAIN: Asturias has three categories in the Sidra de Asturias PDO: *sidra natural, nueva expresión, natural espumosa.*

The Basque Country has Euskal Sagardoa PDO for ciders from Basque region fruit, with an additional *premium* level. There is also *gorenak*, where fruit from outside the Basque region can be included.

sidrería/sagardoteki – cider house in Asturias/Basque Country
terroir – notion that climate, soil, site and culture affect final flavour as well as apple variety and production method
tannins – group of phenols in some fruit which contribute astringency and/or bitterness as well as flavour to cider, with potential to add complexity to a blend; cider-apple varieties have higher tannins than dessert/culinary fruit
traditional method – *see* sparkling cider
transfer method – after a second fermentation in the bottle, instead of riddling and disgorging, the cider is transferred under pressure to a tank, to be separated from its lees before rebottling – *see* sparkling cider
txotx – peg in Basque casks which, when opened, enables sampling; *txotx* season: like a festival every night, a special *txotx* menu accompanies the *txotx* sampling; the head of the cider house holds the *txotx* key
unfined – bottling without filtering

FURTHER READING

Apples of Uncommon Character, Rowan Jacobsen, Bloomsbury USA, 2014

The Botany of Desire, Michael Pollan, Bloomsbury, 2002

Cider, Enthusiasts' Manual, Bill Bradshaw, JH Haynes & Co, 2014

Ciderland, James Crowden, Birlinn Ltd, 2008

Ciderology, Gabe Cook, Spruce, 2018

Craft Cider Making, Andrew Lea, The Crowood Press, 2015

Golden Fire: The Story of Cider, Ted Bruning, New Generation Publishing, 2012

The History and Virtues of Cyder, RK French, Robert Hale, 1982

The New Book of Apples, Joan Morgan and Alison Richards, Ebury Press, 2002

The New Cidermaker's Handbook, Claude Jolicoeur, Chelsea Green, 2013

Tomber Dans Les Pommes, Jean-Pierre Roullaud and Hervé Guirriec, Locus Solus, 2014

Perry Pears, eds LC Luckwill, A Pollard, eds, The National Fruit And Cider Institute, 1963

World's Best Cider, Pete Brown and Bill Bradshaw, Jacqui Small, 2013

INDEX

ACKNOWLEDGEMENTS

What a delight and honour this book has been! So many thank yous to make because this really has been a community effort.

First off, big thanks to Sarah Lavelle and Quadrille for this bold commission. It's both timely and of its time.

Thanks to all who shared tastes, talks and stories. To Tom Oliver, for immense generosity of spirit; Gabe Cook, for passion, dedication and insight; Pete Brown and Bill Bradshaw for *World's Best Cider* (and so much more!); Martin Berkeley; Mike & Albert Johnson; Simon Day; Edwin Winzeler; Felix Nash, for pioneering Fine Cider; Victor Zasadzki. Jackie Denman, for the wonderful Big Apple events; Matt Slocombe.

Chris Losh, my inspirational editor at Imbibe. Steve Lamond, Beoir in Ireland.

In France, the erudite Breton, Mark Gleonec; Ronan Gire, Le Sistrot; Fran Lambert, Atout France, and Carole Rauber, Orne Tourism, who helped make it possible.

In Spain, Anzu Fernándi and the Asturies XXI Foundation family; Basque guide extraordinaire, Haritz Rodriguez, Blog on Brands; Edu Coto, Guerrilla Imports; Daniel Ruiz, Sidra de Asturias, and Unai Agirre, Euskal Sagardoa.

To Michael Stöckl, Cider World and to Kaire Jakobson and Natalia Wszelaki, for European cider chat.

In the dynamic US of A, Ria Windcaller, for her illuminating CiderChat podcasts; Eric West, for warmth, wisdom and unmissable weekly digests; the delightful Darlene Heyes; Michelle McGrath (USACM) for sharing the vibrant enthusiasm of CiderCon; Emily Ritchie (NWCA); Ian Merwin, for his fascinating perspective; Field Maloney, for sharing *The Botany of Desire*. Thanks to Claude Jolicoeur for Canadian insight.

Down Under, thanks to Jane Anderson and Sam Reid at Cider Australia, and Tim Jones, Willie Smith's.

Back to base and a special thank you to my fantastic editor, Sally Somers. Such a treat. To visionary designer Emily Lapworth, talented illustrator Sarah Fisher and the shepherdess herself, Harriet Webster. Apologies to anyone I've missed!

Finally, the biggest thanks to my wonderful husband, James. Without him, none of this would have happened.

Wassail one and all!

PUBLISHING DIRECTOR Sarah Lavelle
EDITORIAL ASSISTANT Harriet Webster
COPY EDITOR Sally Somers
DESIGNER Emily Lapworth
COVER ILLUSTRATION Tom Frost
CIDER ILLUSTRATIONS Sarah Fisher
PRODUCTION Vincent Smith, Jessica Otway, Tom Moore

Published in 2018 by Quadrille, an imprint of Hardie Grant Publishing

Quadrille
52–54 Southwark Street
London SE1 1UN
quadrille.com

Cataloguing in Publication Data: a catalogue record for this book is available from the British Library.

ISBN 978 1 78713 003 6

Printed in China